A 90-Day Self-care and Self-Love Journal

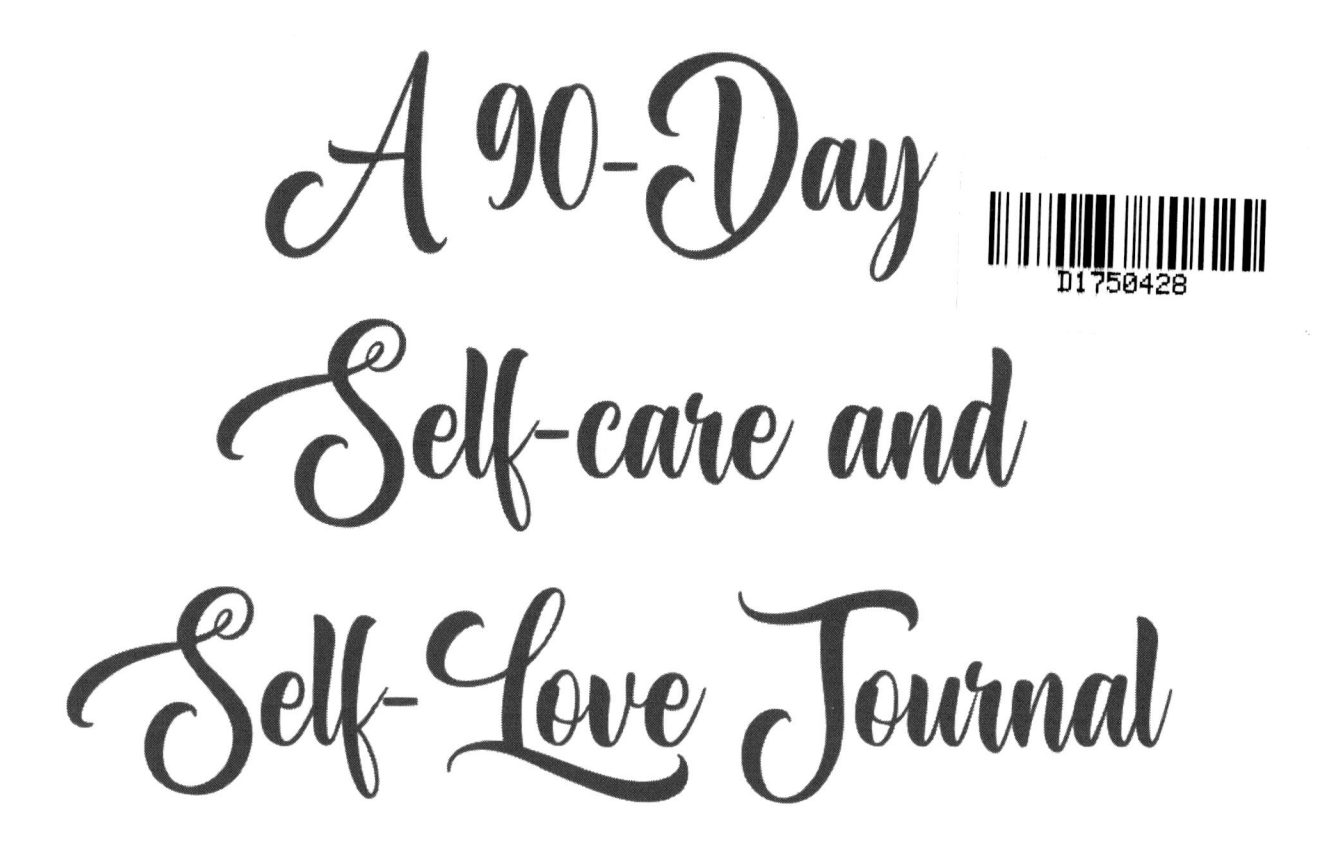

By: Color My Culture

COLOR MY CULTURE

Copyright: 2022 Color My Culture
www.colormyculture.com
ISBN: 978-1-956537-98-7

All rights reserved. No part of this book may be reproduced, stored in a retrieval system, or transmitted by any means, electronic, mechanical, photocopying, recording or otherwise, without the express written permission of the copyright holders.

This Journal belongs To:

All About this Journal.

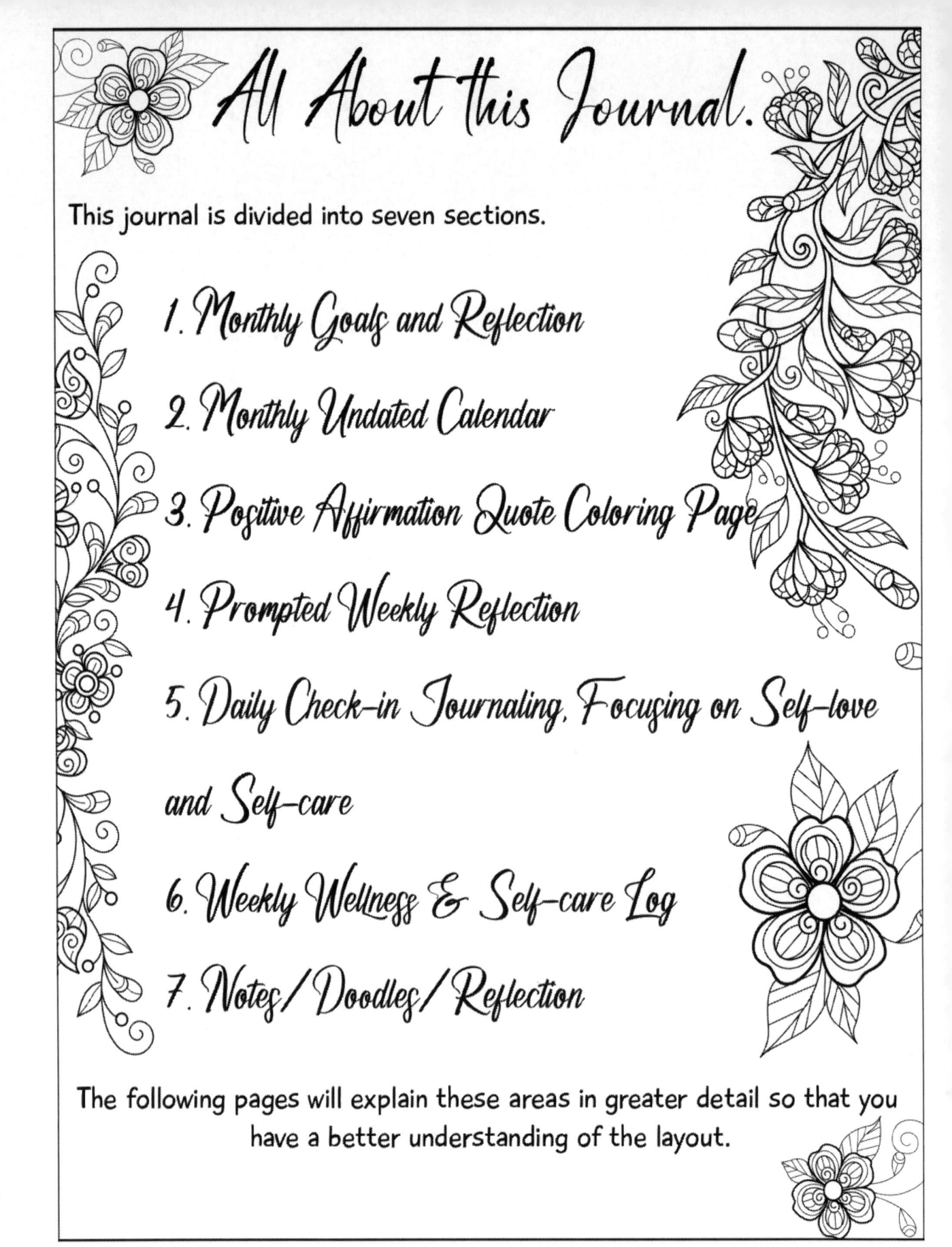

This journal is divided into seven sections.

1. Monthly Goals and Reflection
2. Monthly Undated Calendar
3. Positive Affirmation Quote Coloring Page
4. Prompted Weekly Reflection
5. Daily Check-in Journaling, Focusing on Self-love and Self-care
6. Weekly Wellness & Self-care Log
7. Notes/Doodles/Reflection

The following pages will explain these areas in greater detail so that you have a better understanding of the layout.

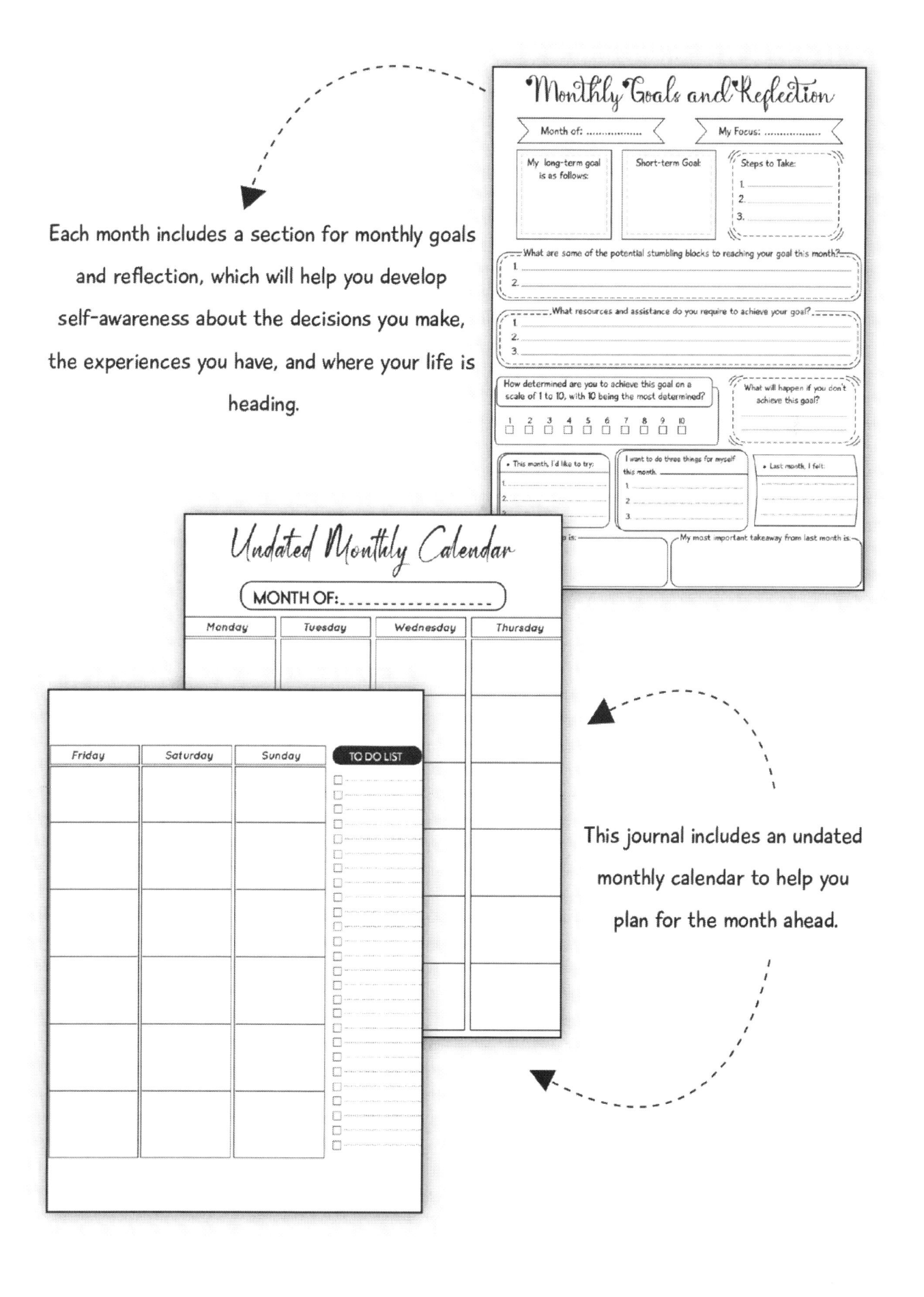

Each month includes a section for monthly goals and reflection, which will help you develop self-awareness about the decisions you make, the experiences you have, and where your life is heading.

This journal includes an undated monthly calendar to help you plan for the month ahead.

Every week, a positive affirmation quote and space to color are provided to help you focus on the positive aspects of your life. Positive affirmations can help you feel better about yourself and your life, take positive action toward your goals, and shift your focus away from the negative and toward the positive. As a form of therapy, coloring can attenuate stress and anxiety, improve concentration, and help you be more present in the moment.

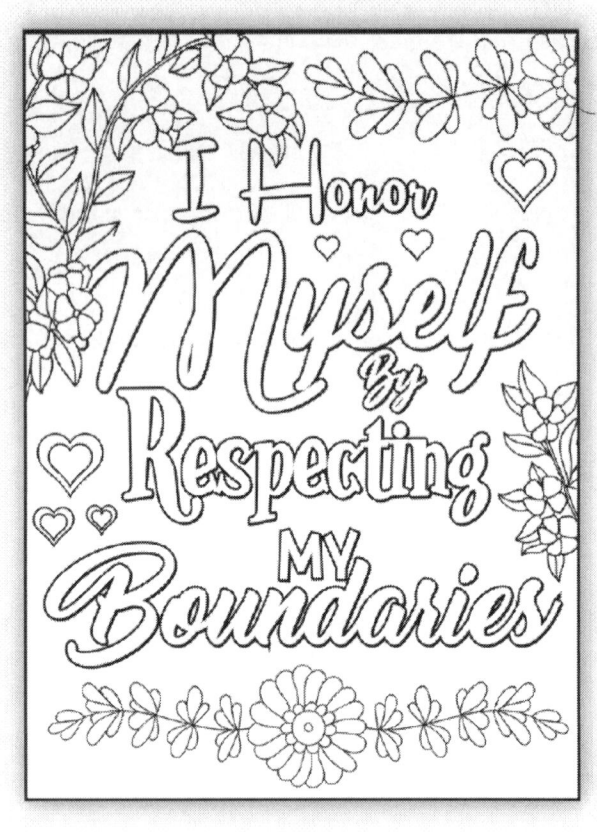

Every week features a new "Reflect" page offering questions and ideas for you to consider, with space provided for you to write down your reactions and reflections.

The daily check-in journaling focuses on self-love and self-care. Every day is a new beginning, a chance to reflect on what went right and wrong.

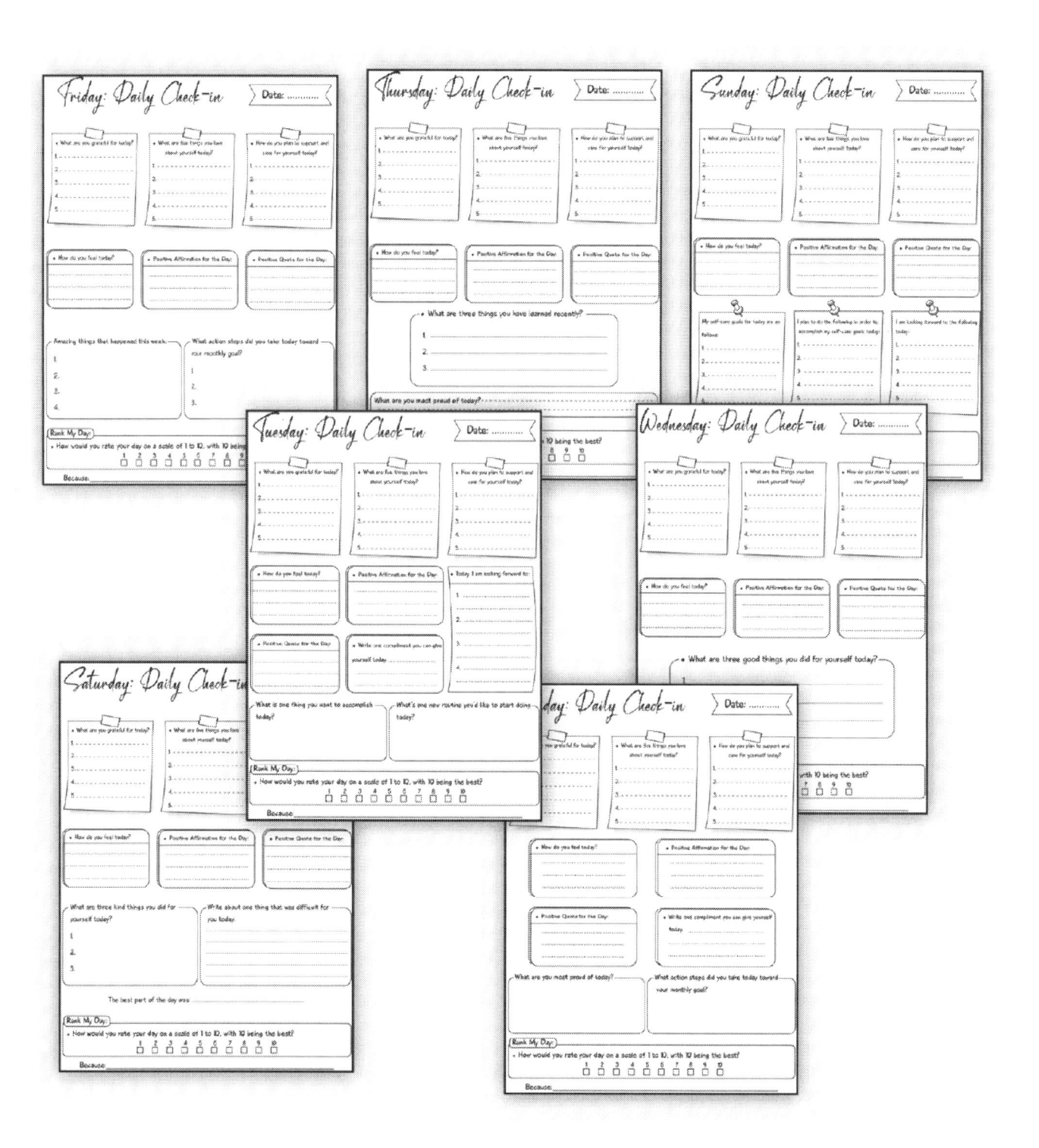

Each week, you'll have a place to keep track of your overall wellness, which includes, mood trackers, fluid consumption, and sleep patterns.

Each week, you have space to take notes, reflect, draw, and doodle. Doodling and drawing can be a meditative and calming experience.

Note: This is your journal. You can complete all sections or just the ones you need.

Self-Care & Self-Love

What is self-care, and how does it connect to self-love? You are most likely familiar with both terms.

Self-love involves accepting and loving yourself unconditionally. It implies that you value yourself, care for yourself, and are kind to yourself. Self-care includes anything you do to minimize stress, focus on your overall well-being, and become your best self. This might be a game, a practice, or a routine. It is something you do on a regular basis and make time for, not just when you are overburdened and stressed out. Is self-care the same as self-love? Some claim that it is, while others argue that, despite their importance, the two are distinct. Self-care is a way of expressing self-love via action. We can care for ourselves without loving ourselves; therefore, self-love is not required for self-care.

Despite their differences, both are necessary for a healthy, contented lifestyle.

Self-Care And Self-Love Inducing Activities

- Try something new
- Go on a nature walk
- Meditate
- Make a vision board
- Connect with friends
- Have a long nap
- Give yourself credit
- Practice deep breathing
- Take your medication
- Plan a fun day out
- Call a family member
- Do something for someone else
- Write in a journal
- Listen to a podcast
- Light a candle
- Gratitude Journaling
- Dance to music
- Eat nourishing food
- Go to a workout class
- Tell yourself "I love you"
- Read a book
- Declutter your living space
- Say yes to something fun
- Buy something that makes you feel good
- Take a break from social media
- Water a plant
- Take a yoga or dance class
- Revisit a childhood hobby
- Unplug from your phone
- Buy yourself flowers
- Visit a bookstore
- Tackle a bad habit
- Do a random act of kindness
- Prayer or meditate for five minutes
- Connect to a mental health professional
- Visit your health care professional
- Call someone you love
- Make your favorite meal
- Wake up 15 minutes earlier
- Stretch for 10-15 minutes
- Listen to your favorite song
- Take yourself on a lunch date
- Clean and orgainize your bed room
- De-clutter a room or desk
- Go to bed 30 minutes earlier
- Read inspirational quotes
- Create your favourite drink
- Drink more water
- Complete a dance workout
- Write down 3 things you that make you smile
- Try a meal you have never tried before
- Go out to lunch with your best friend
- Write a positive letter to future self
- Listen to relaxation music
- Watch a movie or series
- Take a long shower or bath

My Favorites Things

Color: --

Food: ---

Candy: --

Dessert: --

Ice Cream Flavor: -------------------------------

Drink: --

Song: ---

Movie: --

TV Show: --

Place to Eat: -----------------------------------

Person: ---

Season: ---

Holiday: --

Animal: ---

Weekend Activity: -------------------------------

Memory: ---

Scent: --

Book: ---

Sport team: -------------------------------------

My Happy List

Make a list of everything that brightens your day and makes you feel better when you're having a terrible one. For example, listening to your favorite song or reading your favorite book might bring you comfort or happiness when you are having a stressful day.

1. _____
   _____

2. _____
   _____

3. _____
   _____

4. _____
   _____

5. _____
   _____

6. _____
   _____

My Life Story:

What is your life story? Your life story is something that should be written down and maybe shared. Begin by jotting down some biographical information about yourself, such as where you were born, whether you have siblings, a spouse, children, and so on. Some additional questions to consider:

Who are you? What are you really interested in?

Where have you had difficulty? What brings you joy?

Monthly Goals and Reflection

Month of: ....   **My Focus:** ....

My long-term goal is as follows:

Short-term Goal:

Steps to Take:
1. _____
2. _____
3. _____

What are some of the potential stumbling blocks to reaching your goal this month?
1. _____
2. _____

What resources and assistance do you require to achieve your goal?
1. _____
2. _____
3. _____

How determined are you to achieve this goal on a scale of 1 to 10, with 10 being the most determined?

1 ☐ 2 ☐ 3 ☐ 4 ☐ 5 ☐ 6 ☐ 7 ☐ 8 ☐ 9 ☐ 10 ☐

What will happen if you don't achieve this goal?
_____
_____

- **This month, I'd like to try:**
1. ....
2. ....
3. ....

I want to do three things for myself this month.
1. ....
2. ....
3. ....

- **Last month, I felt:**
....
....
....

My monthly recap is:

My most important takeaway from last month is:

Undated Monthly Calendar

MONTH OF: _____

Monday	Tuesday	Wednesday	Thursday

Friday	Saturday	Sunday	**TO DO LIST**

Weekly Wellness & Self-care Log

Mon:	Tue:	Wed:	Thu:
#hours of sleep:	#hours of sleep:	#hours of sleep:	#hours of sleep:
Mood: 😠 ☹️ 😐 🙂 😃	Mood: 😠 ☹️ 😐 🙂 😃	Mood: 😠 ☹️ 😐 🙂 😃	Mood: 😠 ☹️ 😐 🙂 😃
Food: Ⓑ Ⓛ Ⓢ Ⓓ	Food: Ⓑ Ⓛ Ⓢ Ⓓ	Food: Ⓑ Ⓛ Ⓢ Ⓓ	Food: Ⓑ Ⓛ Ⓢ Ⓓ
💧💧💧💧 💧💧💧💧	💧💧💧💧 💧💧💧💧	💧💧💧💧 💧💧💧💧	💧💧💧💧 💧💧💧💧
Self care activity: Workout:	Self care activity: Workout:	Self care activity: Workout:	Self care activity: Workout:

Weekly Wellness & Self-care Log

Fri:	Sat:	Sun:

#hours of sleep:	#hours of sleep:	#hours of sleep:

Mood: ☹ 🙁 😐 🙂 😀	Mood: ☹ 🙁 😐 🙂 😀	Mood: ☹ 🙁 😐 🙂 😀

Food: (B) (L) (S) (D)	Food: (B) (L) (S) (D)	Food: (B) (L) (S) (D)

💧💧💧💧 💧💧💧💧	💧💧💧💧 💧💧💧💧	💧💧💧💧 💧💧💧💧

Self care activity: Workout:	Self care activity: Workout:	Self care activity: Workout:

Weekly Reflection

My Accomplishments

You have numerous reasons to be proud of yourself. Someone who is proud of themselves has a strong sense of self-worth. They frequently have a positive outlook on life, as well as feelings of contentment and gratitude.

You have a lot of positive qualities. Personal characteristics, character traits, skills, or strengths are examples of positive qualities. Many of us find it easier to emphasize the good qualities of others than our own.

You may not realize it, but you have already accomplished a great deal in this life, and you to have the potential to accomplish even more as time passes. Some of us feel embarrassed be proud of our achievements. It is healthy to feel pleased with one's accomplishments. Are you proud of yourself? You ought to be.

1. Compile a list of ten of your accomplishments; it is okay to include achievements from years ago if necessary. Your top ten accomplishments are:

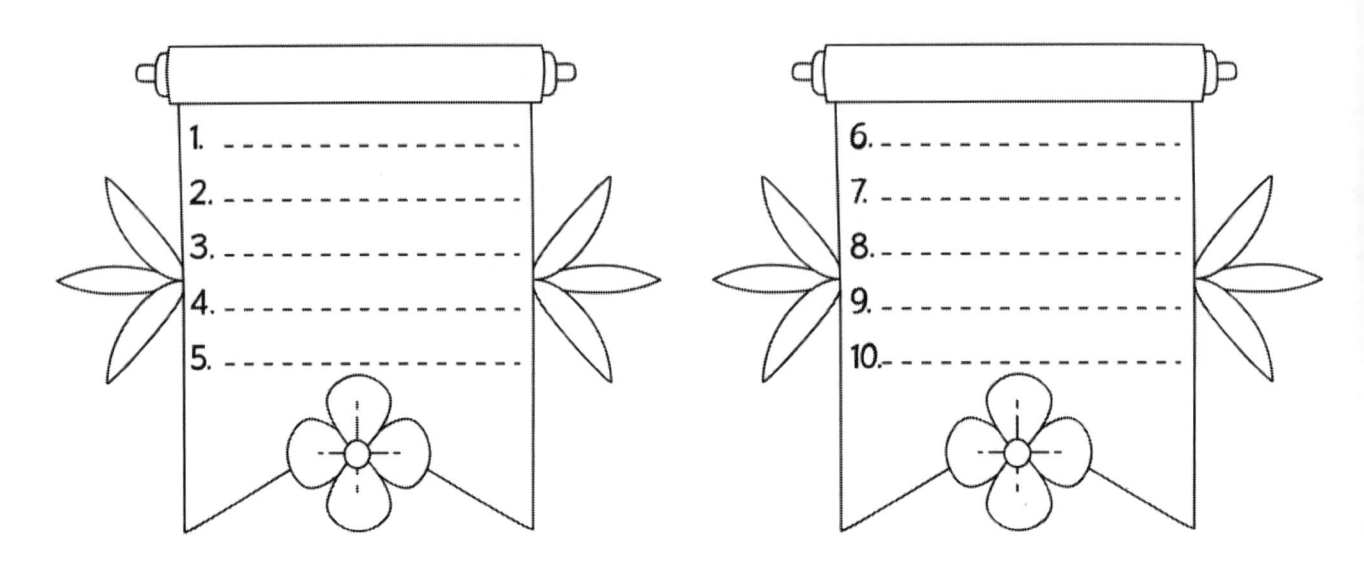

1. _____
2. _____
3. _____
4. _____
5. _____

6. _____
7. _____
8. _____
9. _____
10. _____

2. What are you most proud of yourself for? What makes you unique?

_____
_____
_____
_____

3. What makes you feel powerful?

_____
_____
_____
_____

4. What are some of your positive qualities and best character traits?

_____
_____
_____
_____

Notes/Doodles/Reflection

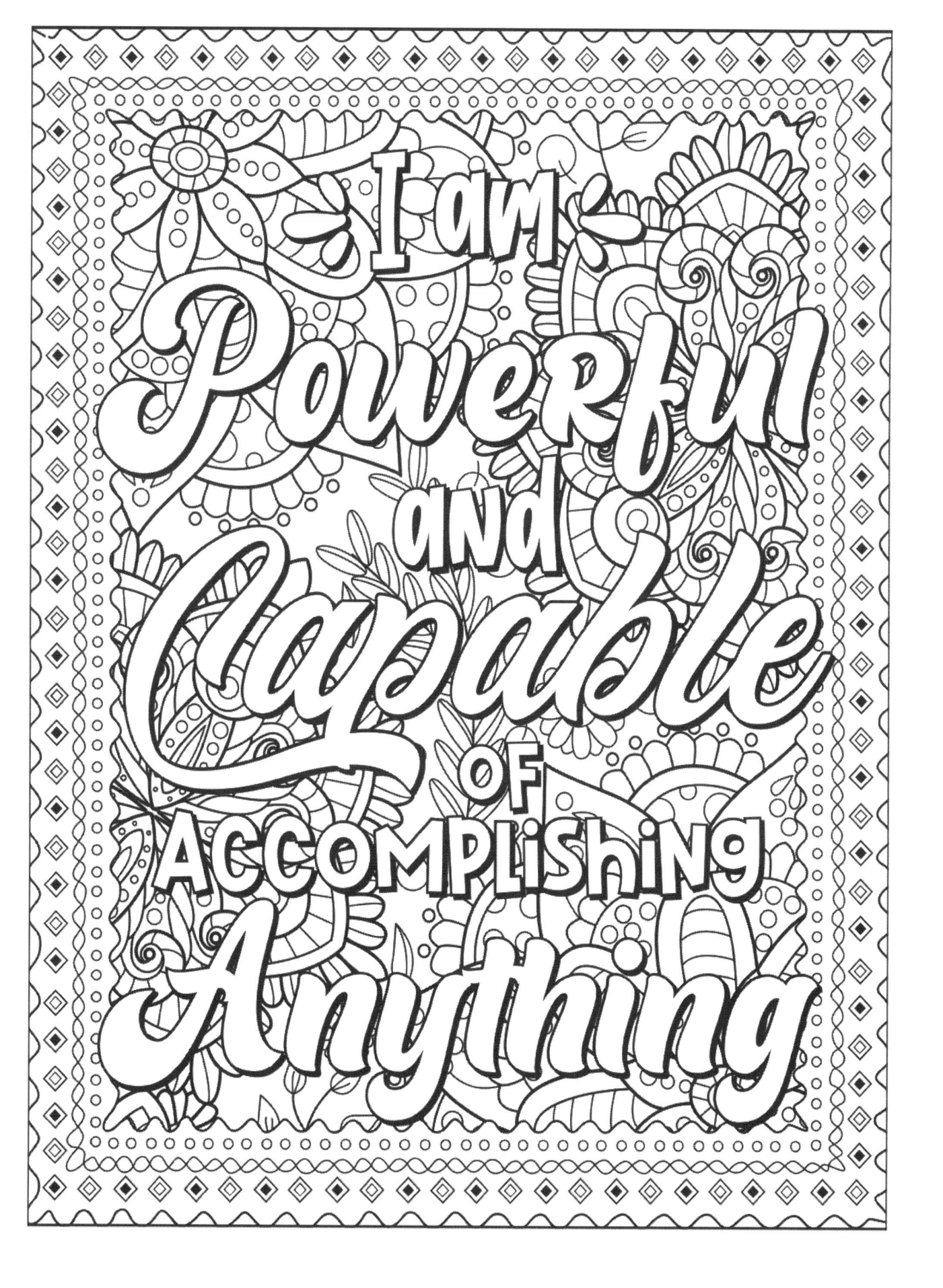

I am Powerful and Capable of Accomplishing Anything

Monday: Daily Check-in

Date: ....

- What are you grateful for today?
  1. - - - - - - - - - - - - - -
  2. - - - - - - - - - - - - - -
  3. - - - - - - - - - - - - - -
  4. - - - - - - - - - - - - - -
  5. - - - - - - - - - - - - - -

- What are five things you love about yourself today?
  1. - - - - - - - - - - - - - - - -
  2. - - - - - - - - - - - - - - - -
  3. - - - - - - - - - - - - - - - -
  4. - - - - - - - - - - - - - - - -
  5. - - - - - - - - - - - - - - - -

- How do you plan to support and care for yourself today?
  1. - - - - - - - - - - - - - - - -
  2. - - - - - - - - - - - - - - - -
  3. - - - - - - - - - - - - - - - -
  4. - - - - - - - - - - - - - - - -
  5. - - - - - - - - - - - - - - - -

- How do you feel today?
  ....
  ....
  ....

- Positive Affirmation for the Day:
  ....
  ....
  ....

- Positive Quote for the Day:
  ....
  ....
  ....

- Write one compliment you can give yourself today. ....
  ....
  ....

What are you most proud of today?

What action steps did you take today toward your monthly goal?

Rank My Day:

- How would you rate your day on a scale of 1 to 10, with 10 being the best?

  1 ☐ 2 ☐ 3 ☐ 4 ☐ 5 ☐ 6 ☐ 7 ☐ 8 ☐ 9 ☐ 10 ☐

Because: _____

Tuesday: Daily Check-in

Date: ....

- What are you grateful for today?
  1. -----------------
  2. -----------------
  3. -----------------
  4. -----------------
  5. -----------------

- What are five things you love about yourself today?
  1. -----------------
  2. -----------------
  3. -----------------
  4. -----------------
  5. -----------------

- How do you plan to support and care for yourself today?
  1. -----------------
  2. -----------------
  3. -----------------
  4. -----------------
  5. -----------------

- How do you feel today?
  ....
  ....
  ....

- Positive Affirmation for the Day:
  ....
  ....
  ....

- Today, I am looking forward to:
  1. ....
  2. ....
  3. ....
  4. ....

- Positive Quote for the Day:
  ....
  ....
  ....

- Write one compliment you can give yourself today. ....
  ....
  ....

What is one thing you want to accomplish today?

What's one new routine you'd like to start doing today?

Rank My Day:

- How would you rate your day on a scale of 1 to 10, with 10 being the best?

  1 ☐ 2 ☐ 3 ☐ 4 ☐ 5 ☐ 6 ☐ 7 ☐ 8 ☐ 9 ☐ 10 ☐

Because:_____

Wednesday: Daily Check-in

Date: ....

- What are you grateful for today?
  1. ----------------
  2. ----------------
  3. ----------------
  4. ----------------
  5. ----------------

- What are five things you love about yourself today?
  1. ----------------
  2. ----------------
  3. ----------------
  4. ----------------
  5. ----------------

- How do you plan to support and care for yourself today?
  1. ----------------
  2. ----------------
  3. ----------------
  4. ----------------
  5. ----------------

- How do you feel today?
  ....
  ....
  ....

- Positive Affirmation for the Day:
  ....
  ....
  ....

- Positive Quote for the Day:
  ....
  ....
  ....

- What are three good things you did for yourself today?
  1. _____
  2. _____
  3. _____

Rank My Day:
- How would you rate your day on a scale of 1 to 10, with 10 being the best?
  1 ☐ 2 ☐ 3 ☐ 4 ☐ 5 ☐ 6 ☐ 7 ☐ 8 ☐ 9 ☐ 10 ☐

Because: _____

Thursday: Daily Check-in

Date: ....

- What are you grateful for today?
  1. _____
  2. _____
  3. _____
  4. _____
  5. _____

- What are five things you love about yourself today?
  1. _____
  2. _____
  3. _____
  4. _____
  5. _____

- How do you plan to support and care for yourself today?
  1. _____
  2. _____
  3. _____
  4. _____
  5. _____

- How do you feel today?
  ....
  ....
  ....

- Positive Affirmation for the Day:
  ....
  ....
  ....

- Positive Quote for the Day:
  ....
  ....
  ....

- What are three things you have learned recently?
  1. _____
  2. _____
  3. _____

What are you most proud of today? _____
_____

Rank My Day:

- How would you rate your day on a scale of 1 to 10, with 10 being the best?

  1 ☐ 2 ☐ 3 ☐ 4 ☐ 5 ☐ 6 ☐ 7 ☐ 8 ☐ 9 ☐ 10 ☐

Because: _____

Friday: Daily Check-in

Date: ....

- What are you grateful for today?
  1. ....
  2. ....
  3. ....
  4. ....
  5. ....

- What are five things you love about yourself today?
  1. ....
  2. ....
  3. ....
  4. ....
  5. ....

- How do you plan to support and care for yourself today?
  1. ....
  2. ....
  3. ....
  4. ....
  5. ....

- How do you feel today?
  ....
  ....
  ....

- Positive Affirmation for the Day:
  ....
  ....
  ....

- Positive Quote for the Day:
  ....
  ....
  ....

Amazing things that happened this week:
1.
2.
3.
4.

What action steps did you take today toward your monthly goal?
1.
2.
3.

Rank My Day:

- How would you rate your day on a scale of 1 to 10, with 10 being the best?

  1 ☐ 2 ☐ 3 ☐ 4 ☐ 5 ☐ 6 ☐ 7 ☐ 8 ☐ 9 ☐ 10 ☐

Because: _____

Saturday: Daily Check-in

Date: ....

- What are you grateful for today?
  1. ----------------------
  2. ----------------------
  3. ----------------------
  4. ----------------------
  5. ----------------------

- What are five things you love about yourself today?
  1. ----------------------
  2. ----------------------
  3. ----------------------
  4. ----------------------
  5. ----------------------

- How do you plan to support and care for yourself today?
  1. ----------------------
  2. ----------------------
  3. ----------------------
  4. ----------------------
  5. ----------------------

- How do you feel today?
  ....
  ....
  ....

- Positive Affirmation for the Day:
  ....
  ....
  ....

- Positive Quote for the Day:
  ....
  ....
  ....

What are three kind things you did for yourself today?
1.
2.
3.

Write about one thing that was difficult for you today.
_____
_____
_____
_____
_____

The best part of the day was: _____

Rank My Day:

- How would you rate your day on a scale of 1 to 10, with 10 being the best?

  1 ☐ 2 ☐ 3 ☐ 4 ☐ 5 ☐ 6 ☐ 7 ☐ 8 ☐ 9 ☐ 10 ☐

Because:_____

Sunday: Daily Check-in

Date: ....

- What are you grateful for today?
  1. _ _ _ _ _ _ _ _ _ _ _ _ _
  2. _ _ _ _ _ _ _ _ _ _ _ _ _
  3. _ _ _ _ _ _ _ _ _ _ _ _ _
  4. _ _ _ _ _ _ _ _ _ _ _ _ _
  5. _ _ _ _ _ _ _ _ _ _ _ _ _

- What are five things you love about yourself today?
  1. _ _ _ _ _ _ _ _ _ _ _ _ _
  2. _ _ _ _ _ _ _ _ _ _ _ _ _
  3. _ _ _ _ _ _ _ _ _ _ _ _ _
  4. _ _ _ _ _ _ _ _ _ _ _ _ _
  5. _ _ _ _ _ _ _ _ _ _ _ _ _

- How do you plan to support and care for yourself today?
  1. _ _ _ _ _ _ _ _ _ _ _ _ _
  2. _ _ _ _ _ _ _ _ _ _ _ _ _
  3. _ _ _ _ _ _ _ _ _ _ _ _ _
  4. _ _ _ _ _ _ _ _ _ _ _ _ _
  5. _ _ _ _ _ _ _ _ _ _ _ _ _

- How do you feel today?

- Positive Affirmation for the Day:

- Positive Quote for the Day:

My self-care goals for today are as follows:
1. _ _ _ _ _ _ _ _ _ _ _ _ _
2. _ _ _ _ _ _ _ _ _ _ _ _ _
3. _ _ _ _ _ _ _ _ _ _ _ _ _
4. _ _ _ _ _ _ _ _ _ _ _ _ _
5. _ _ _ _ _ _ _ _ _ _ _ _ _

I plan to do the following in order to accomplish my self-care goals today:
1. _ _ _ _ _ _ _ _ _ _ _ _ _
2. _ _ _ _ _ _ _ _ _ _ _ _ _
3. _ _ _ _ _ _ _ _ _ _ _ _ _
4. _ _ _ _ _ _ _ _ _ _ _ _ _
5. _ _ _ _ _ _ _ _ _ _ _ _ _

I am looking forward to the following today:
1. _ _ _ _ _ _ _ _ _ _ _ _ _
2. _ _ _ _ _ _ _ _ _ _ _ _ _
3. _ _ _ _ _ _ _ _ _ _ _ _ _
4. _ _ _ _ _ _ _ _ _ _ _ _ _
5. _ _ _ _ _ _ _ _ _ _ _ _ _

Rank My Day:
- How would you rate your day on a scale of 1 to 10, with 10 being the best?

  1 ☐ 2 ☐ 3 ☐ 4 ☐ 5 ☐ 6 ☐ 7 ☐ 8 ☐ 9 ☐ 10 ☐

Because: _____

Weekly Wellness & Self-care Log

Mon:	Tue:	Wed:	Thu:
#hours of sleep:	#hours of sleep:	#hours of sleep:	#hours of sleep:
Mood: 😟 🙁 😐 🙂 😄	Mood: 😟 🙁 😐 🙂 😄	Mood: 😟 🙁 😐 🙂 😄	Mood: 😟 🙁 😐 🙂 😄
Food: Ⓑ Ⓛ Ⓢ Ⓓ	Food: Ⓑ Ⓛ Ⓢ Ⓓ	Food: Ⓑ Ⓛ Ⓢ Ⓓ	Food: Ⓑ Ⓛ Ⓢ Ⓓ
💧💧💧💧 💧💧💧💧	💧💧💧💧 💧💧💧💧	💧💧💧💧 💧💧💧💧	💧💧💧💧 💧💧💧💧
Self care activity: Workout:	Self care activity: Workout:	Self care activity: Workout:	Self care activity: Workout:

Weekly Wellness & Self-care Log

Fri:	Sat:	Sun:
#hours of sleep:	#hours of sleep:	#hours of sleep:
Mood: ☹ 🙁 😐 🙂 😃	Mood: ☹ 🙁 😐 🙂 😃	Mood: ☹ 🙁 😐 🙂 😃
Food: (B) (L) (S) (D)	Food: (B) (L) (S) (D)	Food: (B) (L) (S) (D)
💧💧💧💧 💧💧💧💧	💧💧💧💧 💧💧💧💧	💧💧💧💧 💧💧💧💧
Self care activity: Workout:	Self care activity: Workout:	Self care activity: Workout:

Weekly Reflection

My Authentic Self

Your authentic self transcends the role you play in life, what you do for a living, or what you own. Your authentic self is not influenced by others. It is the core of who you are. It involves being honest to oneself in one's beliefs, words, and deeds. It is an accurate reflection of you.

How would you describe your authentic self?

_____
_____
_____
_____

What are three aspects of your authentic self that you like?

_____
_____
_____
_____

What are three aspects of your authentic self that you don't like but have come to terms with?

_____
_____
_____
_____

How do you accept your authentic self, even if it contradicts the expectations of others?

_____
_____
_____
_____

Notes/Doodles/Reflection

Notes/Doodles/Reflection

It is safe for me to be My Authentic Self

Monday: Daily Check-in

Date: ....

- What are you grateful for today?
  1. _____
  2. _____
  3. _____
  4. _____
  5. _____

- What are five things you love about yourself today?
  1. _____
  2. _____
  3. _____
  4. _____
  5. _____

- How do you plan to support and care for yourself today?
  1. _____
  2. _____
  3. _____
  4. _____
  5. _____

- How do you feel today?
  ....
  ....
  ....

- Positive Affirmation for the Day:
  ....
  ....
  ....

- Positive Quote for the Day:
  ....
  ....
  ....

- Write one compliment you can give yourself today. ....
  ....
  ....

What are you most proud of today?

What action steps did you take today toward your monthly goal?

Rank My Day:

- How would you rate your day on a scale of 1 to 10, with 10 being the best?

  1 ☐ 2 ☐ 3 ☐ 4 ☐ 5 ☐ 6 ☐ 7 ☐ 8 ☐ 9 ☐ 10 ☐

Because: _____

Tuesday: Daily Check-in

Date: ....

- What are you grateful for today?
  1. _____
  2. _____
  3. _____
  4. _____
  5. _____

- What are five things you love about yourself today?
  1. _____
  2. _____
  3. _____
  4. _____
  5. _____

- How do you plan to support and care for yourself today?
  1. _____
  2. _____
  3. _____
  4. _____
  5. _____

- How do you feel today?
  ....
  ....
  ....

- Positive Affirmation for the Day:
  ....
  ....
  ....

- Today, I am looking forward to:
  1. ....
  ....
  2. ....
  ....
  3. ....
  ....
  4. ....
  ....

- Positive Quote for the Day:
  ....
  ....
  ....

- Write one compliment you can give yourself today. ....
  ....
  ....

What is one thing you want to accomplish today?

What's one new routine you'd like to start doing today?

Rank My Day:
- How would you rate your day on a scale of 1 to 10, with 10 being the best?

  1 ☐ 2 ☐ 3 ☐ 4 ☐ 5 ☐ 6 ☐ 7 ☐ 8 ☐ 9 ☐ 10 ☐

Because: _____

Wednesday: Daily Check-in

Date: ....

- What are you grateful for today?
  1. ----------------------
  2. ----------------------
  3. ----------------------
  4. ----------------------
  5. ----------------------

- What are five things you love about yourself today?
  1. ----------------------
  2. ----------------------
  3. ----------------------
  4. ----------------------
  5. ----------------------

- How do you plan to support and care for yourself today?
  1. ----------------------
  2. ----------------------
  3. ----------------------
  4. ----------------------
  5. ----------------------

- How do you feel today?
  ....
  ....
  ....

- Positive Affirmation for the Day:
  ....
  ....
  ....

- Positive Quote for the Day:
  ....
  ....
  ....

- What are three good things you did for yourself today?
  1. _____
  2. _____
  3. _____

Rank My Day:

- How would you rate your day on a scale of 1 to 10, with 10 being the best?

  1 ☐ 2 ☐ 3 ☐ 4 ☐ 5 ☐ 6 ☐ 7 ☐ 8 ☐ 9 ☐ 10 ☐

Because: _____

Thursday: Daily Check-in

Date: ....

• What are you grateful for today?
1. _____
2. _____
3. _____
4. _____
5. _____

• What are five things you love about yourself today?
1. _____
2. _____
3. _____
4. _____
5. _____

• How do you plan to support and care for yourself today?
1. _____
2. _____
3. _____
4. _____
5. _____

• How do you feel today?
....
....
....

• Positive Affirmation for the Day:
....
....
....

• Positive Quote for the Day:
....
....
....

• What are three things you have learned recently?
1. _____
2. _____
3. _____

What are you most proud of today? _____

Rank My Day:
• How would you rate your day on a scale of 1 to 10, with 10 being the best?

1 ☐ 2 ☐ 3 ☐ 4 ☐ 5 ☐ 6 ☐ 7 ☐ 8 ☐ 9 ☐ 10 ☐

Because: _____

Friday: Daily Check-in

Date: ....

- What are you grateful for today?
  1. - - - - - - - - - - - - -
  2. - - - - - - - - - - - - -
  3. - - - - - - - - - - - - -
  4. - - - - - - - - - - - - -
  5. - - - - - - - - - - - - -

- What are five things you love about yourself today?
  1. - - - - - - - - - - - - -
  2. - - - - - - - - - - - - -
  3. - - - - - - - - - - - - -
  4. - - - - - - - - - - - - -
  5. - - - - - - - - - - - - -

- How do you plan to support and care for yourself today?
  1. - - - - - - - - - - - - -
  2. - - - - - - - - - - - - -
  3. - - - - - - - - - - - - -
  4. - - - - - - - - - - - - -
  5. - - - - - - - - - - - - -

- How do you feel today?
  ....
  ....
  ....

- Positive Affirmation for the Day:
  ....
  ....
  ....

- Positive Quote for the Day:
  ....
  ....
  ....

Amazing things that happened this week:
1.
2.
3.
4.

What action steps did you take today toward your monthly goal?
1.
2.
3.

Rank My Day:
- How would you rate your day on a scale of 1 to 10, with 10 being the best?

  1 ☐ 2 ☐ 3 ☐ 4 ☐ 5 ☐ 6 ☐ 7 ☐ 8 ☐ 9 ☐ 10 ☐

Because:_____

Saturday: Daily Check-in

Date: ....

- What are you grateful for today?
  1. ----------------------
  2. ----------------------
  3. ----------------------
  4. ----------------------
  5. ----------------------

- What are five things you love about yourself today?
  1. ----------------------
  2. ----------------------
  3. ----------------------
  4. ----------------------
  5. ----------------------

- How do you plan to support and care for yourself today?
  1. ----------------------
  2. ----------------------
  3. ----------------------
  4. ----------------------
  5. ----------------------

- How do you feel today?

- Positive Affirmation for the Day:

- Positive Quote for the Day:

What are three kind things you did for yourself today?
1.
2.
3.

Write about one thing that was difficult for you today.

The best part of the day was: _____

Rank My Day:

- How would you rate your day on a scale of 1 to 10, with 10 being the best?

  1 ☐ 2 ☐ 3 ☐ 4 ☐ 5 ☐ 6 ☐ 7 ☐ 8 ☐ 9 ☐ 10 ☐

Because: _____

Sunday: Daily Check-in

Date: ....

- What are you grateful for today?
  1. ....
  2. ....
  3. ....
  4. ....
  5. ....

- What are five things you love about yourself today?
  1. ....
  2. ....
  3. ....
  4. ....
  5. ....

- How do you plan to support and care for yourself today?
  1. ....
  2. ....
  3. ....
  4. ....
  5. ....

- How do you feel today?
  ....
  ....
  ....

- Positive Affirmation for the Day:
  ....
  ....
  ....

- Positive Quote for the Day:
  ....
  ....
  ....

My self-care goals for today are as follows:
1. ....
2. ....
3. ....
4. ....
5. ....

I plan to do the following in order to accomplish my self-care goals today:
1. ....
2. ....
3. ....
4. ....
5. ....

I am looking forward to the following today:
1. ....
2. ....
3. ....
4. ....
5. ....

Rank My Day:

- How would you rate your day on a scale of 1 to 10, with 10 being the best?

  1 ☐ 2 ☐ 3 ☐ 4 ☐ 5 ☐ 6 ☐ 7 ☐ 8 ☐ 9 ☐ 10 ☐

Because: _____

Weekly Wellness & Self-care Log

Mon:	Tue:	Wed:	Thu:
#hours of sleep:	#hours of sleep:	#hours of sleep:	#hours of sleep:
Mood: 😠 ☹ 😐 🙂 😀	Mood: 😠 ☹ 😐 🙂 😀	Mood: 😠 ☹ 😐 🙂 😀	Mood: 😠 ☹ 😐 🙂 😀
Food: Ⓑ Ⓛ Ⓢ Ⓓ	Food: Ⓑ Ⓛ Ⓢ Ⓓ	Food: Ⓑ Ⓛ Ⓢ Ⓓ	Food: Ⓑ Ⓛ Ⓢ Ⓓ
💧💧💧💧 💧💧💧💧	💧💧💧💧 💧💧💧💧	💧💧💧💧 💧💧💧💧	💧💧💧💧 💧💧💧💧
Self care activity: Workout:	Self care activity: Workout:	Self care activity: Workout:	Self care activity: Workout:

Weekly Wellness & Self-care Log

Fri:	Sat:	Sun:
#hours of sleep:	#hours of sleep:	#hours of sleep:
Mood: 😟 🙁 😐 🙂 😀	Mood: 😟 🙁 😐 🙂 😀	Mood: 😟 🙁 😐 🙂 😀
Food: Ⓑ Ⓛ Ⓢ Ⓓ	Food: Ⓑ Ⓛ Ⓢ Ⓓ	Food: Ⓑ Ⓛ Ⓢ Ⓓ
💧💧💧💧 💧💧💧💧	💧💧💧💧 💧💧💧💧	💧💧💧💧 💧💧💧💧
Self care activity: Workout:	Self care activity: Workout:	Self care activity: Workout:

Weekly Reflection

Practice Slowing Down

Slowing down entails performing one activity at a time as opposed to moving between multiple things without concentrating fully on any of them. When you slow down, you soon start to savor the present and appreciate the little things in life. We experience less stress as a result. Strategically slowing down isn't always easy, but it is well worth the effort because it promotes both happiness and appreciation for life.

Which part of your life requires you to slow down?

What are some ways you can practice slowing down this week?

Notes/Doodles/Reflection

Notes/Doodles/Reflection

I am scheduling time to enjoy Life

Monday: Daily Check-in

Date: ....

- What are you grateful for today?
1. _ _ _ _ _ _ _ _ _ _ _ _ _ _ _
2. _ _ _ _ _ _ _ _ _ _ _ _ _ _ _
3. _ _ _ _ _ _ _ _ _ _ _ _ _ _ _
4. _ _ _ _ _ _ _ _ _ _ _ _ _ _ _
5. _ _ _ _ _ _ _ _ _ _ _ _ _ _ _

- What are five things you love about yourself today?
1. _ _ _ _ _ _ _ _ _ _ _ _ _ _ _
2. _ _ _ _ _ _ _ _ _ _ _ _ _ _ _
3. _ _ _ _ _ _ _ _ _ _ _ _ _ _ _
4. _ _ _ _ _ _ _ _ _ _ _ _ _ _ _
5. _ _ _ _ _ _ _ _ _ _ _ _ _ _ _

- How do you plan to support and care for yourself today?
1. _ _ _ _ _ _ _ _ _ _ _ _ _ _ _
2. _ _ _ _ _ _ _ _ _ _ _ _ _ _ _
3. _ _ _ _ _ _ _ _ _ _ _ _ _ _ _
4. _ _ _ _ _ _ _ _ _ _ _ _ _ _ _
5. _ _ _ _ _ _ _ _ _ _ _ _ _ _ _

- How do you feel today?
....
....
....

- Positive Affirmation for the Day:
....
....
....

- Positive Quote for the Day:
....
....
....

- Write one compliment you can give yourself today. ....
....
....

What are you most proud of today?

What action steps did you take today toward your monthly goal?

Rank My Day:

- How would you rate your day on a scale of 1 to 10, with 10 being the best?

1 ☐ 2 ☐ 3 ☐ 4 ☐ 5 ☐ 6 ☐ 7 ☐ 8 ☐ 9 ☐ 10 ☐

Because:_____

Tuesday: Daily Check-in

Date: ....

- What are you grateful for today?
  1. _ _ _ _ _ _ _ _ _ _ _ _ _ _ _
  2. _ _ _ _ _ _ _ _ _ _ _ _ _ _ _
  3. _ _ _ _ _ _ _ _ _ _ _ _ _ _ _
  4. _ _ _ _ _ _ _ _ _ _ _ _ _ _ _
  5. _ _ _ _ _ _ _ _ _ _ _ _ _ _ _

- What are five things you love about yourself today?
  1. _ _ _ _ _ _ _ _ _ _ _ _ _ _ _
  2. _ _ _ _ _ _ _ _ _ _ _ _ _ _ _
  3. _ _ _ _ _ _ _ _ _ _ _ _ _ _ _
  4. _ _ _ _ _ _ _ _ _ _ _ _ _ _ _
  5. _ _ _ _ _ _ _ _ _ _ _ _ _ _ _

- How do you plan to support and care for yourself today?
  1. _ _ _ _ _ _ _ _ _ _ _ _ _ _ _
  2. _ _ _ _ _ _ _ _ _ _ _ _ _ _ _
  3. _ _ _ _ _ _ _ _ _ _ _ _ _ _ _
  4. _ _ _ _ _ _ _ _ _ _ _ _ _ _ _
  5. _ _ _ _ _ _ _ _ _ _ _ _ _ _ _

- How do you feel today?
  ....
  ....
  ....

- Positive Affirmation for the Day:
  ....
  ....
  ....

- Today, I am looking forward to:
  1. ....
  ....
  2. ....
  ....
  3. ....
  ....
  4. ....
  ....

- Positive Quote for the Day:
  ....
  ....
  ....

- Write one compliment you can give yourself today. ....
  ....
  ....

What is one thing you want to accomplish today?

What's one new routine you'd like to start doing today?

Rank My Day:

- How would you rate your day on a scale of 1 to 10, with 10 being the best?

  1 ☐ 2 ☐ 3 ☐ 4 ☐ 5 ☐ 6 ☐ 7 ☐ 8 ☐ 9 ☐ 10 ☐

Because: _____

Wednesday: Daily Check-in

Date: ....

- What are you grateful for today?
  1. _____
  2. _____
  3. _____
  4. _____
  5. _____

- What are five things you love about yourself today?
  1. _____
  2. _____
  3. _____
  4. _____
  5. _____

- How do you plan to support and care for yourself today?
  1. _____
  2. _____
  3. _____
  4. _____
  5. _____

- How do you feel today?
  ....
  ....
  ....

- Positive Affirmation for the Day:
  ....
  ....
  ....

- Positive Quote for the Day:
  ....
  ....
  ....

- What are three good things you did for yourself today?
  1. _____
  2. _____
  3. _____

Rank My Day:
- How would you rate your day on a scale of 1 to 10, with 10 being the best?
  1 ☐ 2 ☐ 3 ☐ 4 ☐ 5 ☐ 6 ☐ 7 ☐ 8 ☐ 9 ☐ 10 ☐

Because: _____

Thursday: Daily Check-in

Date: ....

• What are you grateful for today?
1. ----------------
2. ----------------
3. ----------------
4. ----------------
5. ----------------

• What are five things you love about yourself today?
1. ----------------
2. ----------------
3. ----------------
4. ----------------
5. ----------------

• How do you plan to support and care for yourself today?
1. ----------------
2. ----------------
3. ----------------
4. ----------------
5. ----------------

• How do you feel today?
....
....
....

• Positive Affirmation for the Day:
....
....
....

• Positive Quote for the Day:
....
....
....

• What are three things you have learned recently?
1. _____
2. _____
3. _____

What are you most proud of today? ------------------------------
----

Rank My Day:
• How would you rate your day on a scale of 1 to 10, with 10 being the best?

1 ☐ 2 ☐ 3 ☐ 4 ☐ 5 ☐ 6 ☐ 7 ☐ 8 ☐ 9 ☐ 10 ☐

Because: _____

Friday: Daily Check-in

Date: ....

- What are you grateful for today?
  1. ------------------
  2. ------------------
  3. ------------------
  4. ------------------
  5. ------------------

- What are five things you love about yourself today?
  1. ------------------
  2. ------------------
  3. ------------------
  4. ------------------
  5. ------------------

- How do you plan to support and care for yourself today?
  1. ------------------
  2. ------------------
  3. ------------------
  4. ------------------
  5. ------------------

- How do you feel today?

- Positive Affirmation for the Day:

- Positive Quote for the Day:

Amazing things that happened this week:
1.
2.
3.
4.

What action steps did you take today toward your monthly goal?
1.
2.
3.

Rank My Day:
- How would you rate your day on a scale of 1 to 10, with 10 being the best?

  1 ☐ 2 ☐ 3 ☐ 4 ☐ 5 ☐ 6 ☐ 7 ☐ 8 ☐ 9 ☐ 10 ☐

Because:_____

Saturday: Daily Check-in

Date: ....

- What are you grateful for today?
  1. ------------------
  2. ------------------
  3. ------------------
  4. ------------------
  5. ------------------

- What are five things you love about yourself today?
  1. ------------------
  2. ------------------
  3. ------------------
  4. ------------------
  5. ------------------

- How do you plan to support and care for yourself today?
  1. ------------------
  2. ------------------
  3. ------------------
  4. ------------------
  5. ------------------

- How do you feel today?
  ....
  ....
  ....

- Positive Affirmation for the Day:
  ....
  ....
  ....

- Positive Quote for the Day:
  ....
  ....
  ....

What are three kind things you did for yourself today?
1.
2.
3.

Write about one thing that was difficult for you today.
_____
_____
_____
_____
_____

The best part of the day was: _____

Rank My Day:
- How would you rate your day on a scale of 1 to 10, with 10 being the best?

  1 ☐ 2 ☐ 3 ☐ 4 ☐ 5 ☐ 6 ☐ 7 ☐ 8 ☐ 9 ☐ 10 ☐

Because: _____

Sunday: Daily Check-in

Date: ....

- What are you grateful for today?
  1. ----------------------
  2. ----------------------
  3. ----------------------
  4. ----------------------
  5. ----------------------

- What are five things you love about yourself today?
  1. ----------------------
  2. ----------------------
  3. ----------------------
  4. ----------------------
  5. ----------------------

- How do you plan to support and care for yourself today?
  1. ----------------------
  2. ----------------------
  3. ----------------------
  4. ----------------------
  5. ----------------------

- How do you feel today?
  ....
  ....
  ....

- Positive Affirmation for the Day:
  ....
  ....
  ....

- Positive Quote for the Day:
  ....
  ....
  ....

My self-care goals for today are as follows:
1. ----------------------
2. ----------------------
3. ----------------------
4. ----------------------
5. ----------------------

I plan to do the following in order to accomplish my self-care goals today:
1. ----------------------
2. ----------------------
3. ----------------------
4. ----------------------
5. ----------------------

I am looking forward to the following today:
1. ----------------------
2. ----------------------
3. ----------------------
4. ----------------------
5. ----------------------

Rank My Day:
- How would you rate your day on a scale of 1 to 10, with 10 being the best?
  1 ☐ 2 ☐ 3 ☐ 4 ☐ 5 ☐ 6 ☐ 7 ☐ 8 ☐ 9 ☐ 10 ☐

Because: _____

Weekly Wellness & Self-care Log

Mon:	Tue:	Wed:	Thu:
#hours of sleep:	#hours of sleep:	#hours of sleep:	#hours of sleep:
Mood: 😠 ☹️ 😐 🙂 😀	Mood: 😠 ☹️ 😐 🙂 😀	Mood: 😠 ☹️ 😐 🙂 😀	Mood: 😠 ☹️ 😐 🙂 😀
Food: (B) (L) (S) (D)	Food: (B) (L) (S) (D)	Food: (B) (L) (S) (D)	Food: (B) (L) (S) (D)
💧💧💧💧 💧💧💧💧	💧💧💧💧 💧💧💧💧	💧💧💧💧 💧💧💧💧	💧💧💧💧 💧💧💧💧
Self care activity: Workout:	Self care activity: Workout:	Self care activity: Workout:	Self care activity: Workout:

Weekly Wellness & Self-care Log

Fri:	Sat:	Sun:

#hours of sleep: | **#hours of sleep:** | **#hours of sleep:**

Mood: 😟 😕 😐 🙂 😃 | **Mood:** 😟 😕 😐 🙂 😃 | **Mood:** 😟 😕 😐 🙂 😃

Food:
- (B)
- (L)
- (S)
- (D)

Food:
- (B)
- (L)
- (S)
- (D)

Food:
- (B)
- (L)
- (S)
- (D)

💧💧💧💧
💧💧💧💧

💧💧💧💧
💧💧💧💧

💧💧💧💧
💧💧💧💧

Self care activity:

Workout:

Self care activity:

Workout:

Self care activity:

Workout:

Weekly Reflection

My Support System

What is the meaning of a support system? A support system consists of a group of people who are supportive of you, and who provide you with both practical and emotional assistance. Access to a support system has been proven to reduce stress and anxiety and improve one's overall health.

Who is part of your current support system?
_____
_____
_____
_____

How is your current support system set up?
_____
_____
_____
_____

How can you strengthen your support system?
_____
_____
_____
_____

How do you know when you're on the verge of burnout?
_____
_____
_____
_____

What are some of the symptoms and signs of burnout?

_____
_____
_____
_____

How do you ask for help or support when you need it?

_____
_____
_____
_____

Notes/Doodles/Reflection

I am Cherished By my Community

Monday: Daily Check-in

Date: ....

• What are you grateful for today?
1. _ _ _ _ _ _ _ _ _ _ _ _ _ _ _
2. _ _ _ _ _ _ _ _ _ _ _ _ _ _ _
3. _ _ _ _ _ _ _ _ _ _ _ _ _ _ _
4. _ _ _ _ _ _ _ _ _ _ _ _ _ _ _
5. _ _ _ _ _ _ _ _ _ _ _ _ _ _ _

• What are five things you love about yourself today?
1. _ _ _ _ _ _ _ _ _ _ _ _ _ _ _
2. _ _ _ _ _ _ _ _ _ _ _ _ _ _ _
3. _ _ _ _ _ _ _ _ _ _ _ _ _ _ _
4. _ _ _ _ _ _ _ _ _ _ _ _ _ _ _
5. _ _ _ _ _ _ _ _ _ _ _ _ _ _ _

• How do you plan to support and care for yourself today?
1. _ _ _ _ _ _ _ _ _ _ _ _ _ _ _
2. _ _ _ _ _ _ _ _ _ _ _ _ _ _ _
3. _ _ _ _ _ _ _ _ _ _ _ _ _ _ _
4. _ _ _ _ _ _ _ _ _ _ _ _ _ _ _
5. _ _ _ _ _ _ _ _ _ _ _ _ _ _ _

• How do you feel today?
....
....
....

• Positive Affirmation for the Day:
....
....
....

• Positive Quote for the Day:
....
....
....

• Write one compliment you can give yourself today. ....
....
....

What are you most proud of today?

What action steps did you take today toward your monthly goal?

Rank My Day:

• How would you rate your day on a scale of 1 to 10, with 10 being the best?

1 ☐ 2 ☐ 3 ☐ 4 ☐ 5 ☐ 6 ☐ 7 ☐ 8 ☐ 9 ☐ 10 ☐

Because:_____

Tuesday: Daily Check-in

Date: ....

- What are you grateful for today?
  1. ------------------
  2. ------------------
  3. ------------------
  4. ------------------
  5. ------------------

- What are five things you love about yourself today?
  1. ------------------
  2. ------------------
  3. ------------------
  4. ------------------
  5. ------------------

- How do you plan to support and care for yourself today?
  1. ------------------
  2. ------------------
  3. ------------------
  4. ------------------
  5. ------------------

- How do you feel today?
  ....
  ....
  ....

- Positive Affirmation for the Day:
  ....
  ....
  ....

- Today, I am looking forward to:
  1. ....
  ....
  2. ....
  ....
  3. ....
  ....
  4. ....
  ....

- Positive Quote for the Day:
  ....
  ....
  ....

- Write one compliment you can give yourself today. ....
  ....
  ....

What is one thing you want to accomplish today?

What's one new routine you'd like to start doing today?

Rank My Day:

- How would you rate your day on a scale of 1 to 10, with 10 being the best?

  1 ☐ 2 ☐ 3 ☐ 4 ☐ 5 ☐ 6 ☐ 7 ☐ 8 ☐ 9 ☐ 10 ☐

Because: _____

Wednesday: Daily Check-in

Date: ....

- What are you grateful for today?
  1. _ _ _ _ _ _ _ _ _ _ _ _ _
  2. _ _ _ _ _ _ _ _ _ _ _ _ _
  3. _ _ _ _ _ _ _ _ _ _ _ _ _
  4. _ _ _ _ _ _ _ _ _ _ _ _ _
  5. _ _ _ _ _ _ _ _ _ _ _ _ _

- What are five things you love about yourself today?
  1. _ _ _ _ _ _ _ _ _ _ _ _ _ _ _ _ _
  2. _ _ _ _ _ _ _ _ _ _ _ _ _ _ _ _ _
  3. _ _ _ _ _ _ _ _ _ _ _ _ _ _ _ _ _
  4. _ _ _ _ _ _ _ _ _ _ _ _ _ _ _ _ _
  5. _ _ _ _ _ _ _ _ _ _ _ _ _ _ _ _ _

- How do you plan to support and care for yourself today?
  1. _ _ _ _ _ _ _ _ _ _ _ _ _
  2. _ _ _ _ _ _ _ _ _ _ _ _ _
  3. _ _ _ _ _ _ _ _ _ _ _ _ _
  4. _ _ _ _ _ _ _ _ _ _ _ _ _
  5. _ _ _ _ _ _ _ _ _ _ _ _ _

- How do you feel today?

- Positive Affirmation for the Day:

- Positive Quote for the Day:

- What are three good things you did for yourself today?
  1. _____
  2. _____
  3. _____

Rank My Day:
- How would you rate your day on a scale of 1 to 10, with 10 being the best?

  1 ☐ 2 ☐ 3 ☐ 4 ☐ 5 ☐ 6 ☐ 7 ☐ 8 ☐ 9 ☐ 10 ☐

Because:_____

Thursday: Daily Check-in

Date: ....

- What are you grateful for today?
  1. _ _ _ _ _ _ _ _ _ _ _ _ _ _ _
  2. _ _ _ _ _ _ _ _ _ _ _ _ _ _ _
  3. _ _ _ _ _ _ _ _ _ _ _ _ _ _ _
  4. _ _ _ _ _ _ _ _ _ _ _ _ _ _ _
  5. _ _ _ _ _ _ _ _ _ _ _ _ _ _ _

- What are five things you love about yourself today?
  1. _ _ _ _ _ _ _ _ _ _ _ _ _ _ _
  2. _ _ _ _ _ _ _ _ _ _ _ _ _ _ _
  3. _ _ _ _ _ _ _ _ _ _ _ _ _ _ _
  4. _ _ _ _ _ _ _ _ _ _ _ _ _ _ _
  5. _ _ _ _ _ _ _ _ _ _ _ _ _ _ _

- How do you plan to support and care for yourself today?
  1. _ _ _ _ _ _ _ _ _ _ _ _ _ _ _
  2. _ _ _ _ _ _ _ _ _ _ _ _ _ _ _
  3. _ _ _ _ _ _ _ _ _ _ _ _ _ _ _
  4. _ _ _ _ _ _ _ _ _ _ _ _ _ _ _
  5. _ _ _ _ _ _ _ _ _ _ _ _ _ _ _

- How do you feel today?
  ....
  ....
  ....

- Positive Affirmation for the Day:
  ....
  ....
  ....

- Positive Quote for the Day:
  ....
  ....
  ....

- What are three things you have learned recently?
  1. _____
  2. _____
  3. _____

What are you most proud of today? _

Rank My Day:

- How would you rate your day on a scale of 1 to 10, with 10 being the best?

  1 ☐   2 ☐   3 ☐   4 ☐   5 ☐   6 ☐   7 ☐   8 ☐   9 ☐   10 ☐

Because: _____

Friday: Daily Check-in

Date: ....

- What are you grateful for today?
  1. ----------------
  2. ----------------
  3. ----------------
  4. ----------------
  5. ----------------

- What are five things you love about yourself today?
  1. ----------------
  2. ----------------
  3. ----------------
  4. ----------------
  5. ----------------

- How do you plan to support and care for yourself today?
  1. ----------------
  2. ----------------
  3. ----------------
  4. ----------------
  5. ----------------

- How do you feel today?
  ....
  ....
  ....

- Positive Affirmation for the Day:
  ....
  ....
  ....

- Positive Quote for the Day:
  ....
  ....
  ....

Amazing things that happened this week:
1.
2.
3.
4.

What action steps did you take today toward your monthly goal?
1.
2.
3.

Rank My Day:
- How would you rate your day on a scale of 1 to 10, with 10 being the best?

  1 ☐ 2 ☐ 3 ☐ 4 ☐ 5 ☐ 6 ☐ 7 ☐ 8 ☐ 9 ☐ 10 ☐

Because: _____

Saturday: Daily Check-in

Date: ....

- What are you grateful for today?
  1. - - - - - - - - - - - - - - - - -
  2. - - - - - - - - - - - - - - - - -
  3. - - - - - - - - - - - - - - - - -
  4. - - - - - - - - - - - - - - - - -
  5. - - - - - - - - - - - - - - - - -

- What are five things you love about yourself today?
  1. - - - - - - - - - - - - - - - - -
  2. - - - - - - - - - - - - - - - - -
  3. - - - - - - - - - - - - - - - - -
  4. - - - - - - - - - - - - - - - - -
  5. - - - - - - - - - - - - - - - - -

- How do you plan to support and care for yourself today?
  1. - - - - - - - - - - - - - - - - -
  2. - - - - - - - - - - - - - - - - -
  3. - - - - - - - - - - - - - - - - -
  4. - - - - - - - - - - - - - - - - -
  5. - - - - - - - - - - - - - - - - -

- How do you feel today?

- Positive Affirmation for the Day:

- Positive Quote for the Day:

What are three kind things you did for yourself today?
1.
2.
3.

Write about one thing that was difficult for you today.

The best part of the day was: _____

Rank My Day:
- How would you rate your day on a scale of 1 to 10, with 10 being the best?

  1 ☐ 2 ☐ 3 ☐ 4 ☐ 5 ☐ 6 ☐ 7 ☐ 8 ☐ 9 ☐ 10 ☐

Because: _____

Sunday: Daily Check-in

Date: ....

- What are you grateful for today?
  1. -----------------
  2. -----------------
  3. -----------------
  4. -----------------
  5. -----------------

- What are five things you love about yourself today?
  1. -----------------
  2. -----------------
  3. -----------------
  4. -----------------
  5. -----------------

- How do you plan to support and care for yourself today?
  1. -----------------
  2. -----------------
  3. -----------------
  4. -----------------
  5. -----------------

- How do you feel today?
  ....
  ....
  ....

- Positive Affirmation for the Day:
  ....
  ....
  ....

- Positive Quote for the Day:
  ....
  ....
  ....

My self-care goals for today are as follows:
1. -----------------
2. -----------------
3. -----------------
4. -----------------
5. -----------------

I plan to do the following in order to accomplish my self-care goals today:
1. -----------------
2. -----------------
3. -----------------
4. -----------------
5. -----------------

I am looking forward to the following today:
1. -----------------
2. -----------------
3. -----------------
4. -----------------
5. -----------------

Rank My Day:
- How would you rate your day on a scale of 1 to 10, with 10 being the best?
  1 ☐ 2 ☐ 3 ☐ 4 ☐ 5 ☐ 6 ☐ 7 ☐ 8 ☐ 9 ☐ 10 ☐

Because:_____

Monthly Goals and Reflection

Month of: .... **My Focus:** ....

My long-term goal is as follows:

Short-term Goal:

Steps to Take:
1. _____
2. _____
3. _____

What are some of the potential stumbling blocks to reaching your goal this month?
1. _____
2. _____

What resources and assistance do you require to achieve your goal?
1. _____
2. _____
3. _____

How determined are you to achieve this goal on a scale of 1 to 10, with 10 being the most determined?

1 ☐ 2 ☐ 3 ☐ 4 ☐ 5 ☐ 6 ☐ 7 ☐ 8 ☐ 9 ☐ 10 ☐

What will happen if you don't achieve this goal?

- **This month, I'd like to try:**
  1. _____
  2. _____
  3. _____

I want to do three things for myself this month.
1. _____
2. _____
3. _____

- **Last month, I felt:**

My monthly recap is:

My most important takeaway from last month is:

Undated Monthly Calendar

MONTH OF: _____

Monday	Tuesday	Wednesday	Thursday

Friday	Saturday	Sunday	TO DO LIST
			☐ ....
			☐ ....
			☐ ....
			☐ ....
			☐ ....
			☐ ....
			☐ ....
			☐ ....
			☐ ....
			☐ ....
			☐ ....
			☐ ....
			☐ ....
			☐ ....
			☐ ....
			☐ ....
			☐ ....
			☐ ....
			☐ ....
			☐ ....
			☐ ....
			☐ ....
			☐ ....
			☐ ....
			☐ ....

Weekly Wellness & Self-care Log

Mon:	Tue:	Wed:	Thu:
#hours of sleep:	#hours of sleep:	#hours of sleep:	#hours of sleep:
Mood: ☹ 🙁 😐 🙂 😃	Mood: ☹ 🙁 😐 🙂 😃	Mood: ☹ 🙁 😐 🙂 😃	Mood: ☹ 🙁 😐 🙂 😃
Food: (B) (L) (S) (D)	Food: (B) (L) (S) (D)	Food: (B) (L) (S) (D)	Food: (B) (L) (S) (D)
💧💧💧💧 💧💧💧💧	💧💧💧💧 💧💧💧💧	💧💧💧💧 💧💧💧💧	💧💧💧💧 💧💧💧💧
Self care activity: Workout:	Self care activity: Workout:	Self care activity: Workout:	Self care activity: Workout:

Weekly Wellness & Self-care Log

Fri:	Sat:	Sun:
#hours of sleep:	#hours of sleep:	#hours of sleep:
Mood: 😟 😕 😐 🙂 😀	Mood: 😟 😕 😐 🙂 😀	Mood: 😟 😕 😐 🙂 😀
Food: Ⓑ Ⓛ Ⓢ Ⓓ	Food: Ⓑ Ⓛ Ⓢ Ⓓ	Food: Ⓑ Ⓛ Ⓢ Ⓓ
💧💧💧💧 💧💧💧💧	💧💧💧💧 💧💧💧💧	💧💧💧💧 💧💧💧💧
Self care activity: Workout:	Self care activity: Workout:	Self care activity: Workout:

Weekly Reflection

I Love Me

You are the most important person in the whole world to you. You should love and take care of yourself. Think about a person or animal who is important to you. It can be anyone or anything you care about and love. How do you treat this individual or creature? Do you treat them well? How do you approach this individual or creature? Do you approach them with care and respect? What about yourself? Are you treating yourself well? Do you approach yourself with care and love? Self-love starts with the things you do every day.

List three things you do on a regular basis to show yourself love.

_____
_____
_____
_____

What is one thing you do for yourself that makes you happy and calm?

_____
_____
_____
_____

What keeps you from loving yourself to the fullest, and what can you do about it?

_____
_____
_____
_____

This week, list at least three things you can do to show yourself love and kindness.

Notes/Doodles/Reflection

I adore, Accept, and Value Myself and my Talents

Monday: Daily Check-in

Date: ....

- What are you grateful for today?
  1. _ _ _ _ _ _ _ _ _ _ _ _ _
  2. _ _ _ _ _ _ _ _ _ _ _ _ _
  3. _ _ _ _ _ _ _ _ _ _ _ _ _
  4. _ _ _ _ _ _ _ _ _ _ _ _ _
  5. _ _ _ _ _ _ _ _ _ _ _ _ _

- What are five things you love about yourself today?
  1. _ _ _ _ _ _ _ _ _ _ _ _ _
  2. _ _ _ _ _ _ _ _ _ _ _ _ _
  3. _ _ _ _ _ _ _ _ _ _ _ _ _
  4. _ _ _ _ _ _ _ _ _ _ _ _ _
  5. _ _ _ _ _ _ _ _ _ _ _ _ _

- How do you plan to support and care for yourself today?
  1. _ _ _ _ _ _ _ _ _ _ _ _ _
  2. _ _ _ _ _ _ _ _ _ _ _ _ _
  3. _ _ _ _ _ _ _ _ _ _ _ _ _
  4. _ _ _ _ _ _ _ _ _ _ _ _ _
  5. _ _ _ _ _ _ _ _ _ _ _ _ _

- How do you feel today?
  ....
  ....
  ....

- Positive Affirmation for the Day:
  ....
  ....
  ....

- Positive Quote for the Day:
  ....
  ....
  ....

- Write one compliment you can give yourself today. ....
  ....
  ....

What are you most proud of today?

What action steps did you take today toward your monthly goal?

Rank My Day:

- How would you rate your day on a scale of 1 to 10, with 10 being the best?

  1 ☐ 2 ☐ 3 ☐ 4 ☐ 5 ☐ 6 ☐ 7 ☐ 8 ☐ 9 ☐ 10 ☐

Because:_____

Tuesday: Daily Check-in

Date: ....

- What are you grateful for today?
  1. _ _ _ _ _ _ _ _ _ _ _ _ _ _ _
  2. _ _ _ _ _ _ _ _ _ _ _ _ _ _ _
  3. _ _ _ _ _ _ _ _ _ _ _ _ _ _ _
  4. _ _ _ _ _ _ _ _ _ _ _ _ _ _ _
  5. _ _ _ _ _ _ _ _ _ _ _ _ _ _ _

- What are five things you love about yourself today?
  1. _ _ _ _ _ _ _ _ _ _ _ _ _ _ _
  2. _ _ _ _ _ _ _ _ _ _ _ _ _ _ _
  3. _ _ _ _ _ _ _ _ _ _ _ _ _ _ _
  4. _ _ _ _ _ _ _ _ _ _ _ _ _ _ _
  5. _ _ _ _ _ _ _ _ _ _ _ _ _ _ _

- How do you plan to support and care for yourself today?
  1. _ _ _ _ _ _ _ _ _ _ _ _ _ _ _
  2. _ _ _ _ _ _ _ _ _ _ _ _ _ _ _
  3. _ _ _ _ _ _ _ _ _ _ _ _ _ _ _
  4. _ _ _ _ _ _ _ _ _ _ _ _ _ _ _
  5. _ _ _ _ _ _ _ _ _ _ _ _ _ _ _

- How do you feel today?

- Positive Affirmation for the Day:

- Today, I am looking forward to:
  1. ....
  2. ....
  3. ....
  4. ....

- Positive Quote for the Day:

- Write one compliment you can give yourself today. ....

What is one thing you want to accomplish today?

What's one new routine you'd like to start doing today?

Rank My Day:

- How would you rate your day on a scale of 1 to 10, with 10 being the best?

  1 ☐ 2 ☐ 3 ☐ 4 ☐ 5 ☐ 6 ☐ 7 ☐ 8 ☐ 9 ☐ 10 ☐

Because: _____

Wednesday: Daily Check-in

Date: ....

- What are you grateful for today?
  1. -------------------
  2. -------------------
  3. -------------------
  4. -------------------
  5. -------------------

- What are five things you love about yourself today?
  1. -------------------
  2. -------------------
  3. -------------------
  4. -------------------
  5. -------------------

- How do you plan to support and care for yourself today?
  1. -------------------
  2. -------------------
  3. -------------------
  4. -------------------
  5. -------------------

- How do you feel today?
  ....
  ....
  ....

- Positive Affirmation for the Day:
  ....
  ....
  ....

- Positive Quote for the Day:
  ....
  ....
  ....

- What are three good things you did for yourself today?
  1. _____
  2. _____
  3. _____

Rank My Day:
- How would you rate your day on a scale of 1 to 10, with 10 being the best?

  1 ☐ 2 ☐ 3 ☐ 4 ☐ 5 ☐ 6 ☐ 7 ☐ 8 ☐ 9 ☐ 10 ☐

  Because: _____

Thursday: Daily Check-in

Date: ....

- What are you grateful for today?
    1. _____
    2. _____
    3. _____
    4. _____
    5. _____

- What are five things you love about yourself today?
    1. _____
    2. _____
    3. _____
    4. _____
    5. _____

- How do you plan to support and care for yourself today?
    1. _____
    2. _____
    3. _____
    4. _____
    5. _____

- How do you feel today?
    ....
    ....
    ....

- Positive Affirmation for the Day:
    ....
    ....
    ....

- Positive Quote for the Day:
    ....
    ....
    ....

- What are three things you have learned recently?
    1. _____
    2. _____
    3. _____

What are you most proud of today? _____
_____

Rank My Day:
- How would you rate your day on a scale of 1 to 10, with 10 being the best?

    1 2 3 4 5 6 7 8 9 10
    ☐ ☐ ☐ ☐ ☐ ☐ ☐ ☐ ☐ ☐

Because: _____

Friday: Daily Check-in

Date: ....

- What are you grateful for today?
  1. ---------------------
  2. ---------------------
  3. ---------------------
  4. ---------------------
  5. ---------------------

- What are five things you love about yourself today?
  1. ---------------------
  2. ---------------------
  3. ---------------------
  4. ---------------------
  5. ---------------------

- How do you plan to support and care for yourself today?
  1. ---------------------
  2. ---------------------
  3. ---------------------
  4. ---------------------
  5. ---------------------

- How do you feel today?
  ....
  ....
  ....

- Positive Affirmation for the Day:
  ....
  ....
  ....

- Positive Quote for the Day:
  ....
  ....
  ....

Amazing things that happened this week:
1.
2.
3.
4.

What action steps did you take today toward your monthly goal?
1.
2.
3.

Rank My Day:

- How would you rate your day on a scale of 1 to 10, with 10 being the best?

  1 ☐ 2 ☐ 3 ☐ 4 ☐ 5 ☐ 6 ☐ 7 ☐ 8 ☐ 9 ☐ 10 ☐

Because: _____

Saturday: Daily Check-in

Date: ....

- What are you grateful for today?
  1. _____
  2. _____
  3. _____
  4. _____
  5. _____

- What are five things you love about yourself today?
  1. _____
  2. _____
  3. _____
  4. _____
  5. _____

- How do you plan to support and care for yourself today?
  1. _____
  2. _____
  3. _____
  4. _____
  5. _____

- How do you feel today?
  ....
  ....
  ....

- Positive Affirmation for the Day:
  ....
  ....
  ....

- Positive Quote for the Day:
  ....
  ....
  ....

What are three kind things you did for yourself today?
1.
2.
3.

Write about one thing that was difficult for you today.
_____
_____
_____
_____
_____

The best part of the day was: _____

Rank My Day:
- How would you rate your day on a scale of 1 to 10, with 10 being the best?

  1 ☐ 2 ☐ 3 ☐ 4 ☐ 5 ☐ 6 ☐ 7 ☐ 8 ☐ 9 ☐ 10 ☐

Because: _____

Sunday: Daily Check-in

Date: ....

- What are you grateful for today?
  1. _____
  2. _____
  3. _____
  4. _____
  5. _____

- What are five things you love about yourself today?
  1. _____
  2. _____
  3. _____
  4. _____
  5. _____

- How do you plan to support and care for yourself today?
  1. _____
  2. _____
  3. _____
  4. _____
  5. _____

- How do you feel today?
  ....
  ....
  ....

- Positive Affirmation for the Day:
  ....
  ....
  ....

- Positive Quote for the Day:
  ....
  ....
  ....

My self-care goals for today are as follows:
1. _____
2. _____
3. _____
4. _____
5. _____

I plan to do the following in order to accomplish my self-care goals today:
1. _____
2. _____
3. _____
4. _____
5. _____

I am looking forward to the following today:
1. _____
2. _____
3. _____
4. _____
5. _____

Rank My Day:

- How would you rate your day on a scale of 1 to 10, with 10 being the best?

  1 ☐ 2 ☐ 3 ☐ 4 ☐ 5 ☐ 6 ☐ 7 ☐ 8 ☐ 9 ☐ 10 ☐

Because: _____

Weekly Wellness & Self-care Log

Mon:	Tue:	Wed:	Thu:
#hours of sleep:	#hours of sleep:	#hours of sleep:	#hours of sleep:
Mood: 😠 😟 😐 🙂 😄	Mood: 😠 😟 😐 🙂 😄	Mood: 😠 😟 😐 🙂 😄	Mood: 😠 😟 😐 🙂 😄
Food: ⓑ ⓛ ⓢ ⓓ	Food: ⓑ ⓛ ⓢ ⓓ	Food: ⓑ ⓛ ⓢ ⓓ	Food: ⓑ ⓛ ⓢ ⓓ
💧💧💧💧 💧💧💧💧	💧💧💧💧 💧💧💧💧	💧💧💧💧 💧💧💧💧	💧💧💧💧 💧💧💧💧
Self care activity: Workout:	Self care activity: Workout:	Self care activity: Workout:	Self care activity: Workout:

Weekly Wellness & Self-care Log

Fri:	Sat:	Sun:
#hours of sleep:	#hours of sleep:	#hours of sleep:
Mood: ☹ 😐 😑 🙂 😃	Mood: ☹ 😐 😑 🙂 😃	Mood: ☹ 😐 😑 🙂 😃
Food: Ⓑ Ⓛ Ⓢ Ⓓ	Food: Ⓑ Ⓛ Ⓢ Ⓓ	Food: Ⓑ Ⓛ Ⓢ Ⓓ
💧💧💧💧 💧💧💧💧	💧💧💧💧 💧💧💧💧	💧💧💧💧 💧💧💧💧
Self care activity: Workout:	Self care activity: Workout:	Self care activity: Workout:

Weekly Reflection

My Boundaries

What exactly does the term "boundaries" mean? Boundaries assist you in determining what you are comfortable with and how you want others to treat you. They entail respecting your needs, emotions, and thoughts. Boundaries are necessary in relationships with friends, family, coworkers, a partner, and even strangers. It is necessary to know where you stand and communicate it to others, to maintain social harmony and equilibrium. Your boundaries reflect your most important values.

If you're unsure about your boundaries, consider your personal space, your values, and your basic rights. Consider where and when you typically feel safe. Do you have any established boundaries?

_____
_____
_____
_____
_____
_____

List at least three of your current boundaries.

_____
_____
_____
_____

How do you maintain your boundaries?

What is one new healthy boundary you can set in your life today?

How do you plan to implement this healthy boundary in your relationship and your life as a whole?

Notes/Doodles/Reflection

I Honor Myself By Respecting My Boundaries

Monday: Daily Check-in

Date: ....

- What are you grateful for today?
  1. _ _ _ _ _ _ _ _ _ _ _ _ _ _
  2. _ _ _ _ _ _ _ _ _ _ _ _ _ _
  3. _ _ _ _ _ _ _ _ _ _ _ _ _ _
  4. _ _ _ _ _ _ _ _ _ _ _ _ _ _
  5. _ _ _ _ _ _ _ _ _ _ _ _ _ _

- What are five things you love about yourself today?
  1. _ _ _ _ _ _ _ _ _ _ _ _ _ _
  2. _ _ _ _ _ _ _ _ _ _ _ _ _ _
  3. _ _ _ _ _ _ _ _ _ _ _ _ _ _
  4. _ _ _ _ _ _ _ _ _ _ _ _ _ _
  5. _ _ _ _ _ _ _ _ _ _ _ _ _ _

- How do you plan to support and care for yourself today?
  1. _ _ _ _ _ _ _ _ _ _ _ _ _ _
  2. _ _ _ _ _ _ _ _ _ _ _ _ _ _
  3. _ _ _ _ _ _ _ _ _ _ _ _ _ _
  4. _ _ _ _ _ _ _ _ _ _ _ _ _ _
  5. _ _ _ _ _ _ _ _ _ _ _ _ _ _

- How do you feel today?

  ....
  ....
  ....

- Positive Affirmation for the Day:

  ....
  ....
  ....

- Positive Quote for the Day:

  ....
  ....
  ....

- Write one compliment you can give yourself today. ....
  ....
  ....

What are you most proud of today?

What action steps did you take today toward your monthly goal?

Rank My Day:

- How would you rate your day on a scale of 1 to 10, with 10 being the best?

  1 ☐ 2 ☐ 3 ☐ 4 ☐ 5 ☐ 6 ☐ 7 ☐ 8 ☐ 9 ☐ 10 ☐

Because: _____

Tuesday: Daily Check-in

Date: ....

- What are you grateful for today?
  1. - - - - - - - - - - - - - - - -
  2. - - - - - - - - - - - - - - - -
  3. - - - - - - - - - - - - - - - -
  4. - - - - - - - - - - - - - - - -
  5. - - - - - - - - - - - - - - - -

- What are five things you love about yourself today?
  1. - - - - - - - - - - - - - - - -
  2. - - - - - - - - - - - - - - - -
  3. - - - - - - - - - - - - - - - -
  4. - - - - - - - - - - - - - - - -
  5. - - - - - - - - - - - - - - - -

- How do you plan to support and care for yourself today?
  1. - - - - - - - - - - - - - - - -
  2. - - - - - - - - - - - - - - - -
  3. - - - - - - - - - - - - - - - -
  4. - - - - - - - - - - - - - - - -
  5. - - - - - - - - - - - - - - - -

- How do you feel today?

- Positive Affirmation for the Day:

- Today, I am looking forward to:
  1. ....
  2. ....
  3. ....
  4. ....

- Positive Quote for the Day:

- Write one compliment you can give yourself today. ....

- What is one thing you want to accomplish today?

- What's one new routine you'd like to start doing today?

Rank My Day:
- How would you rate your day on a scale of 1 to 10, with 10 being the best?

  1 ☐ 2 ☐ 3 ☐ 4 ☐ 5 ☐ 6 ☐ 7 ☐ 8 ☐ 9 ☐ 10 ☐

Because: _____

Wednesday: Daily Check-in

Date: ....

- What are you grateful for today?
  1. -------------------
  2. -------------------
  3. -------------------
  4. -------------------
  5. -------------------

- What are five things you love about yourself today?
  1. -------------------
  2. -------------------
  3. -------------------
  4. -------------------
  5. -------------------

- How do you plan to support and care for yourself today?
  1. -------------------
  2. -------------------
  3. -------------------
  4. -------------------
  5. -------------------

- How do you feel today?
  ....
  ....
  ....

- Positive Affirmation for the Day:
  ....
  ....
  ....

- Positive Quote for the Day:
  ....
  ....
  ....

- What are three good things you did for yourself today?
  1. _____
  2. _____
  3. _____

Rank My Day:

- How would you rate your day on a scale of 1 to 10, with 10 being the best?

  1 ☐ 2 ☐ 3 ☐ 4 ☐ 5 ☐ 6 ☐ 7 ☐ 8 ☐ 9 ☐ 10 ☐

Because:_____

Thursday: Daily Check-in

Date: ....

- What are you grateful for today?
  1. _____
  2. _____
  3. _____
  4. _____
  5. _____

- What are five things you love about yourself today?
  1. _____
  2. _____
  3. _____
  4. _____
  5. _____

- How do you plan to support and care for yourself today?
  1. _____
  2. _____
  3. _____
  4. _____
  5. _____

- How do you feel today?
  ....
  ....
  ....

- Positive Affirmation for the Day:
  ....
  ....
  ....

- Positive Quote for the Day:
  ....
  ....
  ....

- What are three things you have learned recently?
  1. _____
  2. _____
  3. _____

What are you most proud of today? _____

Rank My Day:
- How would you rate your day on a scale of 1 to 10, with 10 being the best?
  1 ☐ 2 ☐ 3 ☐ 4 ☐ 5 ☐ 6 ☐ 7 ☐ 8 ☐ 9 ☐ 10 ☐

Because: _____

Friday: Daily Check-in

Date: ....

- What are you grateful for today?
  1. - - - - - - - - - - - - - -
  2. - - - - - - - - - - - - - -
  3. - - - - - - - - - - - - - -
  4. - - - - - - - - - - - - - -
  5. - - - - - - - - - - - - - -

- What are five things you love about yourself today?
  1. - - - - - - - - - - - - - -
  2. - - - - - - - - - - - - - -
  3. - - - - - - - - - - - - - -
  4. - - - - - - - - - - - - - -
  5. - - - - - - - - - - - - - -

- How do you plan to support and care for yourself today?
  1. - - - - - - - - - - - - - -
  2. - - - - - - - - - - - - - -
  3. - - - - - - - - - - - - - -
  4. - - - - - - - - - - - - - -
  5. - - - - - - - - - - - - - -

- How do you feel today?
  ....
  ....
  ....

- Positive Affirmation for the Day:
  ....
  ....
  ....

- Positive Quote for the Day:
  ....
  ....
  ....

Amazing things that happened this week:
1.
2.
3.
4.

What action steps did you take today toward your monthly goal?
1.
2.
3.

Rank My Day:

- How would you rate your day on a scale of 1 to 10, with 10 being the best?

  1 ☐ 2 ☐ 3 ☐ 4 ☐ 5 ☐ 6 ☐ 7 ☐ 8 ☐ 9 ☐ 10 ☐

Because:_____

Saturday: Daily Check-in

Date: ....

- What are you grateful for today?
  1. ------------------------
  2. ------------------------
  3. ------------------------
  4. ------------------------
  5. ------------------------

- What are five things you love about yourself today?
  1. ------------------------
  2. ------------------------
  3. ------------------------
  4. ------------------------
  5. ------------------------

- How do you plan to support and care for yourself today?
  1. ------------------------
  2. ------------------------
  3. ------------------------
  4. ------------------------
  5. ------------------------

- How do you feel today?
  ....
  ....
  ....

- Positive Affirmation for the Day:
  ....
  ....
  ....

- Positive Quote for the Day:
  ....
  ....
  ....

What are three kind things you did for yourself today?
1.
2.
3.

Write about one thing that was difficult for you today.
_____
_____
_____
_____
_____

The best part of the day was: _____

Rank My Day:
- How would you rate your day on a scale of 1 to 10, with 10 being the best?

  1 ☐ 2 ☐ 3 ☐ 4 ☐ 5 ☐ 6 ☐ 7 ☐ 8 ☐ 9 ☐ 10 ☐

Because: _____

Sunday: Daily Check-in

Date: ....

- What are you grateful for today?
  1. _____
  2. _____
  3. _____
  4. _____
  5. _____

- What are five things you love about yourself today?
  1. _____
  2. _____
  3. _____
  4. _____
  5. _____

- How do you plan to support and care for yourself today?
  1. _____
  2. _____
  3. _____
  4. _____
  5. _____

- How do you feel today?
  ....
  ....
  ....

- Positive Affirmation for the Day:
  ....
  ....
  ....

- Positive Quote for the Day:
  ....
  ....
  ....

My self-care goals for today are as follows:
1. _____
2. _____
3. _____
4. _____
5. _____

I plan to do the following in order to accomplish my self-care goals today:
1. _____
2. _____
3. _____
4. _____
5. _____

I am looking forward to the following today:
1. _____
2. _____
3. _____
4. _____
5. _____

Rank My Day:

- How would you rate your day on a scale of 1 to 10, with 10 being the best?
  1 ☐ 2 ☐ 3 ☐ 4 ☐ 5 ☐ 6 ☐ 7 ☐ 8 ☐ 9 ☐ 10 ☐

Because: _____

Weekly Wellness & Self-care Log

Mon:	Tue:	Wed:	Thu:
#hours of sleep:	#hours of sleep:	#hours of sleep:	#hours of sleep:
Mood: 😠 😟 😐 🙂 😃	Mood: 😠 😟 😐 🙂 😃	Mood: 😠 😟 😐 🙂 😃	Mood: 😠 😟 😐 🙂 😃
Food: Ⓑ Ⓛ Ⓢ Ⓓ	Food: Ⓑ Ⓛ Ⓢ Ⓓ	Food: Ⓑ Ⓛ Ⓢ Ⓓ	Food: Ⓑ Ⓛ Ⓢ Ⓓ
💧💧💧💧 💧💧💧💧	💧💧💧💧 💧💧💧💧	💧💧💧💧 💧💧💧💧	💧💧💧💧 💧💧💧💧
Self care activity: Workout:	Self care activity: Workout:	Self care activity: Workout:	Self care activity: Workout:

Weekly Wellness & Self-care Log

Fri:	Sat:	Sun:
#hours of sleep:	#hours of sleep:	#hours of sleep:
Mood: ☹ 🙁 😐 🙂 😃	Mood: ☹ 🙁 😐 🙂 😃	Mood: ☹ 🙁 😐 🙂 😃
Food: Ⓑ Ⓛ Ⓢ Ⓓ	Food: Ⓑ Ⓛ Ⓢ Ⓓ	Food: Ⓑ Ⓛ Ⓢ Ⓓ
💧💧💧💧 💧💧💧💧	💧💧💧💧 💧💧💧💧	💧💧💧💧 💧💧💧💧
Self care activity: Workout:	Self care activity: Workout:	Self care activity: Workout:

Weekly Reflection

My People

Spending time with those who matter to us can bring positive joy into our lives. Quality time spent with family and friends can reduce the likelihood of developing anxiety, depression, and other mental illnesses. It also provides you a greater feeling of belonging and purpose, and aids you in coping with trauma and other adversities.

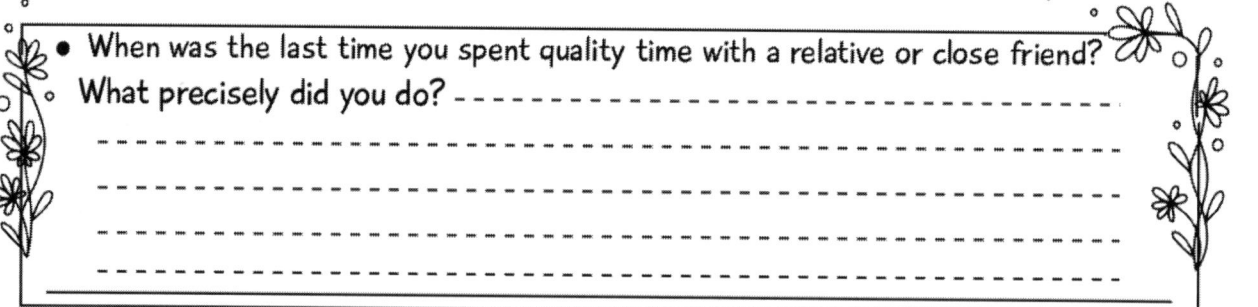

- When was the last time you spent quality time with a relative or close friend? What precisely did you do?

- How did you feel about it?

- How can you improve the intentionality of your interactions with others?

- How do you communicate your feelings to those who care for you?

Notes/Doodles/Reflection

Notes/Doodles/Reflection

I am CURRENTLY Enjoying the people in MY Life

Monday: Daily Check-in

Date: ....

- What are you grateful for today?
  1. _ _ _ _ _ _ _ _ _ _ _ _ _ _ _
  2. _ _ _ _ _ _ _ _ _ _ _ _ _ _ _
  3. _ _ _ _ _ _ _ _ _ _ _ _ _ _ _
  4. _ _ _ _ _ _ _ _ _ _ _ _ _ _ _
  5. _ _ _ _ _ _ _ _ _ _ _ _ _ _ _

- What are five things you love about yourself today?
  1. _ _ _ _ _ _ _ _ _ _ _ _ _ _ _
  2. _ _ _ _ _ _ _ _ _ _ _ _ _ _ _
  3. _ _ _ _ _ _ _ _ _ _ _ _ _ _ _
  4. _ _ _ _ _ _ _ _ _ _ _ _ _ _ _
  5. _ _ _ _ _ _ _ _ _ _ _ _ _ _ _

- How do you plan to support and care for yourself today?
  1. _ _ _ _ _ _ _ _ _ _ _ _ _ _ _
  2. _ _ _ _ _ _ _ _ _ _ _ _ _ _ _
  3. _ _ _ _ _ _ _ _ _ _ _ _ _ _ _
  4. _ _ _ _ _ _ _ _ _ _ _ _ _ _ _
  5. _ _ _ _ _ _ _ _ _ _ _ _ _ _ _

- How do you feel today?

- Positive Affirmation for the Day:

- Positive Quote for the Day:

- Write one compliment you can give yourself today. ....

What are you most proud of today?

What action steps did you take today toward your monthly goal?

Rank My Day:

- How would you rate your day on a scale of 1 to 10, with 10 being the best?

  1 ☐ 2 ☐ 3 ☐ 4 ☐ 5 ☐ 6 ☐ 7 ☐ 8 ☐ 9 ☐ 10 ☐

Because: _____

Tuesday: Daily Check-in

Date: ....

- What are you grateful for today?
  1. _____
  2. _____
  3. _____
  4. _____
  5. _____

- What are five things you love about yourself today?
  1. _____
  2. _____
  3. _____
  4. _____
  5. _____

- How do you plan to support and care for yourself today?
  1. _____
  2. _____
  3. _____
  4. _____
  5. _____

- How do you feel today?
  ....
  ....
  ....

- Positive Affirmation for the Day:
  ....
  ....
  ....

- Today, I am looking forward to:
  1. ....
  2. ....
  3. ....
  4. ....

- Positive Quote for the Day:
  ....
  ....
  ....

- Write one compliment you can give yourself today. ....
  ....
  ....

What is one thing you want to accomplish today?

What's one new routine you'd like to start doing today?

Rank My Day:

- How would you rate your day on a scale of 1 to 10, with 10 being the best?

  1 ☐ 2 ☐ 3 ☐ 4 ☐ 5 ☐ 6 ☐ 7 ☐ 8 ☐ 9 ☐ 10 ☐

Because: _____

Wednesday: Daily Check-in

Date: ....

- What are you grateful for today?
  1. _____
  2. _____
  3. _____
  4. _____
  5. _____

- What are five things you love about yourself today?
  1. _____
  2. _____
  3. _____
  4. _____
  5. _____

- How do you plan to support and care for yourself today?
  1. _____
  2. _____
  3. _____
  4. _____
  5. _____

- How do you feel today?
  ....
  ....
  ....

- Positive Affirmation for the Day:
  ....
  ....
  ....

- Positive Quote for the Day:
  ....
  ....
  ....

- What are three good things you did for yourself today?
  1. _____
  2. _____
  3. _____

Rank My Day:

- How would you rate your day on a scale of 1 to 10, with 10 being the best?

  1 ☐ 2 ☐ 3 ☐ 4 ☐ 5 ☐ 6 ☐ 7 ☐ 8 ☐ 9 ☐ 10 ☐

Because: _____

Thursday: Daily Check-in

Date: ....

- What are you grateful for today?
  1. ------------------------
  2. ------------------------
  3. ------------------------
  4. ------------------------
  5. ------------------------

- What are five things you love about yourself today?
  1. ------------------------
  2. ------------------------
  3. ------------------------
  4. ------------------------
  5. ------------------------

- How do you plan to support and care for yourself today?
  1. ------------------------
  2. ------------------------
  3. ------------------------
  4. ------------------------
  5. ------------------------

- How do you feel today?
  ....
  ....
  ....

- Positive Affirmation for the Day:
  ....
  ....
  ....

- Positive Quote for the Day:
  ....
  ....
  ....

- What are three things you have learned recently?
  1. _____
  2. _____
  3. _____

What are you most proud of today? ------------------------------
----

Rank My Day:

- How would you rate your day on a scale of 1 to 10, with 10 being the best?

  1 ☐ 2 ☐ 3 ☐ 4 ☐ 5 ☐ 6 ☐ 7 ☐ 8 ☐ 9 ☐ 10 ☐

Because: _____

Friday: Daily Check-in

Date: ....

- What are you grateful for today?
  1. ------------------
  2. ------------------
  3. ------------------
  4. ------------------
  5. ------------------

- What are five things you love about yourself today?
  1. ------------------
  2. ------------------
  3. ------------------
  4. ------------------
  5. ------------------

- How do you plan to support and care for yourself today?
  1. ------------------
  2. ------------------
  3. ------------------
  4. ------------------
  5. ------------------

- How do you feel today?

- Positive Affirmation for the Day:

- Positive Quote for the Day:

Amazing things that happened this week:
1.
2.
3.
4.

What action steps did you take today toward your monthly goal?
1.
2.
3.

Rank My Day:

- How would you rate your day on a scale of 1 to 10, with 10 being the best?

  1 ☐ 2 ☐ 3 ☐ 4 ☐ 5 ☐ 6 ☐ 7 ☐ 8 ☐ 9 ☐ 10 ☐

Because: _____

Saturday: Daily Check-in

Date: ....

- What are you grateful for today?
  1. _____
  2. _____
  3. _____
  4. _____
  5. _____

- What are five things you love about yourself today?
  1. _____
  2. _____
  3. _____
  4. _____
  5. _____

- How do you plan to support and care for yourself today?
  1. _____
  2. _____
  3. _____
  4. _____
  5. _____

- How do you feel today?
  ....
  ....
  ....

- Positive Affirmation for the Day:
  ....
  ....
  ....

- Positive Quote for the Day:
  ....
  ....
  ....

What are three kind things you did for yourself today?
1.
2.
3.

Write about one thing that was difficult for you today.
_____
_____
_____
_____
_____

The best part of the day was: _____

Rank My Day:
- How would you rate your day on a scale of 1 to 10, with 10 being the best?

  1 ☐ 2 ☐ 3 ☐ 4 ☐ 5 ☐ 6 ☐ 7 ☐ 8 ☐ 9 ☐ 10 ☐

Because:_____

Sunday: Daily Check-in

Date: ....

- What are you grateful for today?
  1. ....
  2. ....
  3. ....
  4. ....
  5. ....

- What are five things you love about yourself today?
  1. ....
  2. ....
  3. ....
  4. ....
  5. ....

- How do you plan to support and care for yourself today?
  1. ....
  2. ....
  3. ....
  4. ....
  5. ....

- How do you feel today?
  ....
  ....
  ....

- Positive Affirmation for the Day:
  ....
  ....
  ....

- Positive Quote for the Day:
  ....
  ....
  ....

My self-care goals for today are as follows:
1. ....
2. ....
3. ....
4. ....
5. ....

I plan to do the following in order to accomplish my self-care goals today:
1. ....
2. ....
3. ....
4. ....
5. ....

I am looking forward to the following today:
1. ....
2. ....
3. ....
4. ....
5. ....

Rank My Day:
- How would you rate your day on a scale of 1 to 10, with 10 being the best?
  1 ☐ 2 ☐ 3 ☐ 4 ☐ 5 ☐ 6 ☐ 7 ☐ 8 ☐ 9 ☐ 10 ☐

Because: _____

Weekly Wellness & Self-care Log

Mon:	Tue:	Wed:	Thu:
#hours of sleep:	#hours of sleep:	#hours of sleep:	#hours of sleep:
Mood: 😠 ☹️ 😐 🙂 😃	Mood: 😠 ☹️ 😐 🙂 😃	Mood: 😠 ☹️ 😐 🙂 😃	Mood: 😠 ☹️ 😐 🙂 😃
Food: Ⓑ Ⓛ Ⓢ Ⓓ	Food: Ⓑ Ⓛ Ⓢ Ⓓ	Food: Ⓑ Ⓛ Ⓢ Ⓓ	Food: Ⓑ Ⓛ Ⓢ Ⓓ
💧💧💧💧 💧💧💧💧	💧💧💧💧 💧💧💧💧	💧💧💧💧 💧💧💧💧	💧💧💧💧 💧💧💧💧
Self care activity: Workout:	Self care activity: Workout:	Self care activity: Workout:	Self care activity: Workout:

Weekly Wellness & Self-care Log

Fri:	Sat:	Sun:
#hours of sleep:	#hours of sleep:	#hours of sleep:
Mood: ☹ 🙁 😐 🙂 😀	Mood: ☹ 🙁 😐 🙂 😀	Mood: ☹ 🙁 😐 🙂 😀
Food: (B) (L) (S) (D)	Food: (B) (L) (S) (D)	Food: (B) (L) (S) (D)
💧💧💧💧 💧💧💧💧	💧💧💧💧 💧💧💧💧	💧💧💧💧 💧💧💧💧
Self care activity: Workout:	Self care activity: Workout:	Self care activity: Workout:

Weekly Reflection

My Life Change

There are numerous sayings about having only one life to live. We only have one chance at life, so we should make it the best we can. Do you believe that you're living the best life possible? There are aspects of our lives that we have control over and can alter to live the life we choose. What aspect of your life do you believe requires modification so that you can live the best life possible? Perhaps you are unhappy with your finances, your weight, your health, your relationships, your job, or your community. For instance, if you are dissatisfied with your finances, what can you do to improve that aspect of your life? How do you envision your financial future?

What are you dissatisfied with in your life? Prior to making any changes in your life, you should determine what you do not want your life to become before attempting to make any changes. Then, you can decide what you want to change to move closer to the life you want, and you can also learn to value and protect your own energy.

- So, what aspects of your life must you change to live the best life possible?

- What is one change you can make to live the best possible life?

- What specific steps can you take to make this transformation a reality?

- How do you motivate yourself to attempt something new?

Notes/Doodles/Reflection

The only person who can Change Me is MySelf No one Else

Monday: Daily Check-in

Date: ....

- What are you grateful for today?
  1. _ _ _ _ _ _ _ _ _ _ _ _ _ _ _
  2. _ _ _ _ _ _ _ _ _ _ _ _ _ _ _
  3. _ _ _ _ _ _ _ _ _ _ _ _ _ _ _
  4. _ _ _ _ _ _ _ _ _ _ _ _ _ _ _
  5. _ _ _ _ _ _ _ _ _ _ _ _ _ _ _

- What are five things you love about yourself today?
  1. _ _ _ _ _ _ _ _ _ _ _ _ _ _ _
  2. _ _ _ _ _ _ _ _ _ _ _ _ _ _ _
  3. _ _ _ _ _ _ _ _ _ _ _ _ _ _ _
  4. _ _ _ _ _ _ _ _ _ _ _ _ _ _ _
  5. _ _ _ _ _ _ _ _ _ _ _ _ _ _ _

- How do you plan to support and care for yourself today?
  1. _ _ _ _ _ _ _ _ _ _ _ _ _ _ _
  2. _ _ _ _ _ _ _ _ _ _ _ _ _ _ _
  3. _ _ _ _ _ _ _ _ _ _ _ _ _ _ _
  4. _ _ _ _ _ _ _ _ _ _ _ _ _ _ _
  5. _ _ _ _ _ _ _ _ _ _ _ _ _ _ _

- How do you feel today?

- Positive Affirmation for the Day:

- Positive Quote for the Day:

- Write one compliment you can give yourself today.

What are you most proud of today?

What action steps did you take today toward your monthly goal?

(Rank My Day:)

- How would you rate your day on a scale of 1 to 10, with 10 being the best?

  1 ☐ 2 ☐ 3 ☐ 4 ☐ 5 ☐ 6 ☐ 7 ☐ 8 ☐ 9 ☐ 10 ☐

Because: _____

Tuesday: Daily Check-in

Date: ....

- What are you grateful for today?
  1. - - - - - - - - - - - - - - - - -
  2. - - - - - - - - - - - - - - - - -
  3. - - - - - - - - - - - - - - - - -
  4. - - - - - - - - - - - - - - - - -
  5. - - - - - - - - - - - - - - - - -

- What are five things you love about yourself today?
  1. - - - - - - - - - - - - - - - - -
  2. - - - - - - - - - - - - - - - - -
  3. - - - - - - - - - - - - - - - - -
  4. - - - - - - - - - - - - - - - - -
  5. - - - - - - - - - - - - - - - - -

- How do you plan to support and care for yourself today?
  1. - - - - - - - - - - - - - - - - -
  2. - - - - - - - - - - - - - - - - -
  3. - - - - - - - - - - - - - - - - -
  4. - - - - - - - - - - - - - - - - -
  5. - - - - - - - - - - - - - - - - -

- How do you feel today?

- Positive Affirmation for the Day:

- Today, I am looking forward to:
  1. ....
  2. ....
  3. ....
  4. ....

- Positive Quote for the Day:

- Write one compliment you can give yourself today. ....

What is one thing you want to accomplish today?

What's one new routine you'd like to start doing today?

Rank My Day:
- How would you rate your day on a scale of 1 to 10, with 10 being the best?

  1 ☐ 2 ☐ 3 ☐ 4 ☐ 5 ☐ 6 ☐ 7 ☐ 8 ☐ 9 ☐ 10 ☐

Because: _____

Wednesday: Daily Check-in

Date: ....

- What are you grateful for today?
  1. ....
  2. ....
  3. ....
  4. ....
  5. ....

- What are five things you love about yourself today?
  1. ....
  2. ....
  3. ....
  4. ....
  5. ....

- How do you plan to support and care for yourself today?
  1. ....
  2. ....
  3. ....
  4. ....
  5. ....

- How do you feel today?
  ....
  ....
  ....

- Positive Affirmation for the Day:
  ....
  ....
  ....

- Positive Quote for the Day:
  ....
  ....
  ....

- What are three good things you did for yourself today?
  1. _____
  2. _____
  3. _____

Rank My Day:

- How would you rate your day on a scale of 1 to 10, with 10 being the best?

  1 ☐ 2 ☐ 3 ☐ 4 ☐ 5 ☐ 6 ☐ 7 ☐ 8 ☐ 9 ☐ 10 ☐

Because: _____

Thursday: Daily Check-in

Date: ....

- What are you grateful for today?
  1. _____
  2. _____
  3. _____
  4. _____
  5. _____

- What are five things you love about yourself today?
  1. _____
  2. _____
  3. _____
  4. _____
  5. _____

- How do you plan to support and care for yourself today?
  1. _____
  2. _____
  3. _____
  4. _____
  5. _____

- How do you feel today?
  ....
  ....
  ....

- Positive Affirmation for the Day:
  ....
  ....
  ....

- Positive Quote for the Day:
  ....
  ....
  ....

- What are three things you have learned recently?
  1. _____
  2. _____
  3. _____

What are you most proud of today? _____
_____

Rank My Day:
- How would you rate your day on a scale of 1 to 10, with 10 being the best?

  1 ☐ 2 ☐ 3 ☐ 4 ☐ 5 ☐ 6 ☐ 7 ☐ 8 ☐ 9 ☐ 10 ☐

Because: _____

Friday: Daily Check-in

Date: ....

- What are you grateful for today?
    1. ------------------
    2. ------------------
    3. ------------------
    4. ------------------
    5. ------------------

- What are five things you love about yourself today?
    1. ------------------
    2. ------------------
    3. ------------------
    4. ------------------
    5. ------------------

- How do you plan to support and care for yourself today?
    1. ------------------
    2. ------------------
    3. ------------------
    4. ------------------
    5. ------------------

- How do you feel today?
    ....
    ....
    ....

- Positive Affirmation for the Day:
    ....
    ....
    ....

- Positive Quote for the Day:
    ....
    ....
    ....

Amazing things that happened this week:
1.
2.
3.
4.

What action steps did you take today toward your monthly goal?
1.
2.
3.

Rank My Day:
- How would you rate your day on a scale of 1 to 10, with 10 being the best?

    1 ☐ 2 ☐ 3 ☐ 4 ☐ 5 ☐ 6 ☐ 7 ☐ 8 ☐ 9 ☐ 10 ☐

Because: _____

Saturday: Daily Check-in

Date: ....

- What are you grateful for today?
  1. ------------------
  2. ------------------
  3. ------------------
  4. ------------------
  5. ------------------

- What are five things you love about yourself today?
  1. ------------------
  2. ------------------
  3. ------------------
  4. ------------------
  5. ------------------

- How do you plan to support and care for yourself today?
  1. ------------------
  2. ------------------
  3. ------------------
  4. ------------------
  5. ------------------

- How do you feel today?
  ....
  ....
  ....

- Positive Affirmation for the Day:
  ....
  ....
  ....

- Positive Quote for the Day:
  ....
  ....
  ....

What are three kind things you did for yourself today?
1.
2.
3.

Write about one thing that was difficult for you today.
_____
_____
_____
_____
_____

The best part of the day was: _____

Rank My Day:

- How would you rate your day on a scale of 1 to 10, with 10 being the best?

  1 ☐ 2 ☐ 3 ☐ 4 ☐ 5 ☐ 6 ☐ 7 ☐ 8 ☐ 9 ☐ 10 ☐

Because: _____

Sunday: Daily Check-in

Date: ....

- What are you grateful for today?
  1. _____
  2. _____
  3. _____
  4. _____
  5. _____

- What are five things you love about yourself today?
  1. _____
  2. _____
  3. _____
  4. _____
  5. _____

- How do you plan to support and care for yourself today?
  1. _____
  2. _____
  3. _____
  4. _____
  5. _____

- How do you feel today?
  ....
  ....
  ....

- Positive Affirmation for the Day:
  ....
  ....
  ....

- Positive Quote for the Day:
  ....
  ....
  ....

My self-care goals for today are as follows:
  1. _____
  2. _____
  3. _____
  4. _____
  5. _____

I plan to do the following in order to accomplish my self-care goals today:
  1. _____
  2. _____
  3. _____
  4. _____
  5. _____

I am looking forward to the following today:
  1. _____
  2. _____
  3. _____
  4. _____
  5. _____

Rank My Day:

- How would you rate your day on a scale of 1 to 10, with 10 being the best?

  1 ☐   2 ☐   3 ☐   4 ☐   5 ☐   6 ☐   7 ☐   8 ☐   9 ☐   10 ☐

Because:_____

Monthly Goals and Reflection

Month of: ....   **My Focus:** ....

My long-term goal is as follows:

Short-term Goal:

Steps to Take:
1. _____
2. _____
3. _____

What are some of the potential stumbling blocks to reaching your goal this month?
1. _____
2. _____

What resources and assistance do you require to achieve your goal?
1. _____
2. _____
3. _____

How determined are you to achieve this goal on a scale of 1 to 10, with 10 being the most determined?

1 ☐ 2 ☐ 3 ☐ 4 ☐ 5 ☐ 6 ☐ 7 ☐ 8 ☐ 9 ☐ 10 ☐

What will happen if you don't achieve this goal?
_____
_____

- **This month, I'd like to try:**
1. ....
2. ....
3. ....

I want to do three things for myself this month.
1. ....
2. ....
3. ....

- **Last month, I felt:**
....
....
....

My monthly recap is:

My most important takeaway from last month is:

Undated Monthly Calendar

MONTH OF: _

Monday	Tuesday	Wednesday	Thursday

Friday	Saturday	Sunday	**TO DO LIST**
			☐ ....
			☐ ....
			☐ ....
			☐ ....
			☐ ....
			☐ ....
			☐ ....
			☐ ....
			☐ ....
			☐ ....
			☐ ....
			☐ ....
			☐ ....
			☐ ....
			☐ ....
			☐ ....
			☐ ....
			☐ ....
			☐ ....
			☐ ....
			☐ ....
			☐ ....
			☐ ....
			☐ ....
			☐ ....
			☐ ....

Weekly Wellness & Self-care Log

Mon:	Tue:	Wed:	Thu:
#hours of sleep:	#hours of sleep:	#hours of sleep:	#hours of sleep:
Mood: 😠 ☹️ 😐 🙂 😃	Mood: 😠 ☹️ 😐 🙂 😃	Mood: 😠 ☹️ 😐 🙂 😃	Mood: 😠 ☹️ 😐 🙂 😃
Food: Ⓑ Ⓛ Ⓢ Ⓓ	Food: Ⓑ Ⓛ Ⓢ Ⓓ	Food: Ⓑ Ⓛ Ⓢ Ⓓ	Food: Ⓑ Ⓛ Ⓢ Ⓓ
💧💧💧💧 💧💧💧💧	💧💧💧💧 💧💧💧💧	💧💧💧💧 💧💧💧💧	💧💧💧💧 💧💧💧💧
Self care activity: Workout:	Self care activity: Workout:	Self care activity: Workout:	Self care activity: Workout:

Weekly Wellness & Self-care Log

Fri:	Sat:	Sun:
#hours of sleep:	#hours of sleep:	#hours of sleep:
Mood: 😦 😕 😐 🙂 😃	Mood: 😦 😕 😐 🙂 😃	Mood: 😦 😕 😐 🙂 😃
Food: Ⓑ Ⓛ Ⓢ Ⓓ	Food: Ⓑ Ⓛ Ⓢ Ⓓ	Food: Ⓑ Ⓛ Ⓢ Ⓓ
💧💧💧💧 💧💧💧💧	💧💧💧💧 💧💧💧💧	💧💧💧💧 💧💧💧💧
Self care activity: Workout:	Self care activity: Workout:	Self care activity: Workout:

Weekly Reflection

My Needs

Some of us have never been taught what we need to feel safe, loved, and cared for. Some of us did not grow up in a place where we felt loved, safe, and secure, all of which are basic needs. Because of this, some of us don't think we deserve this experience.

For this reason, some of us are drawn to people who are bad for us.

When we place what we think are our needs first, we feel bad about it. In some situations, it might be okay to put the needs of those you love ahead of your own, but there should be a balance. You can only give other people so much of yourself, so set clear limits and make sure that giving yourself doesn't hurt your health or well-being. When you're burned out, you can't help yourself or anyone else.

- What do you need to feel safe, loved, and in control?
  _____
  _____
  _____
  _____

- What needs to happen to make you feel safe and secure in life?
  _____
  _____
  _____
  _____

- What would it be like to have meaning, autonomy, and identity in your life?
  _____
  _____
  _____
  _____

- Are you communicating your needs to your family and friends? If so, how? _____
_____
_____
_____

- Do you consider your current method of communicating your needs to be effective? _____
_____
_____
_____

- In what ways do you prioritize the needs of others over your own?
_____
_____
_____
_____

Notes/Doodles/Reflection

I am The Highest Priority in My Life

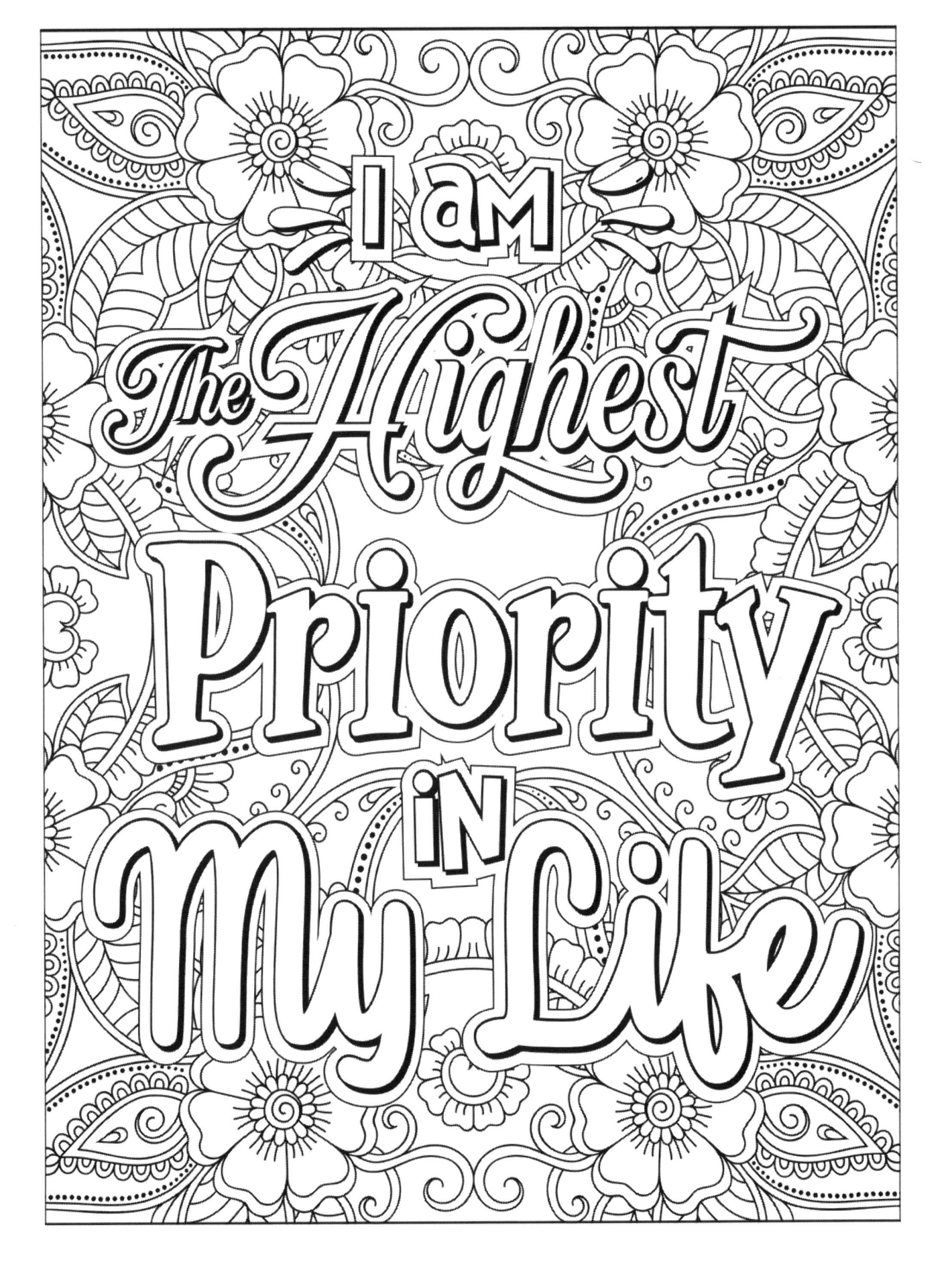

Monday: Daily Check-in

Date: ....

- What are you grateful for today?
  1. _ _ _ _ _ _ _ _ _ _ _ _ _ _
  2. _ _ _ _ _ _ _ _ _ _ _ _ _ _
  3. _ _ _ _ _ _ _ _ _ _ _ _ _ _
  4. _ _ _ _ _ _ _ _ _ _ _ _ _ _
  5. _ _ _ _ _ _ _ _ _ _ _ _ _ _

- What are five things you love about yourself today?
  1. _ _ _ _ _ _ _ _ _ _ _ _ _ _ _ _ _
  2. _ _ _ _ _ _ _ _ _ _ _ _ _ _ _ _ _
  3. _ _ _ _ _ _ _ _ _ _ _ _ _ _ _ _ _
  4. _ _ _ _ _ _ _ _ _ _ _ _ _ _ _ _ _
  5. _ _ _ _ _ _ _ _ _ _ _ _ _ _ _ _ _

- How do you plan to support and care for yourself today?
  1. _ _ _ _ _ _ _ _ _ _ _ _ _ _ _ _ _
  2. _ _ _ _ _ _ _ _ _ _ _ _ _ _ _ _ _
  3. _ _ _ _ _ _ _ _ _ _ _ _ _ _ _ _ _
  4. _ _ _ _ _ _ _ _ _ _ _ _ _ _ _ _ _
  5. _ _ _ _ _ _ _ _ _ _ _ _ _ _ _ _ _

- How do you feel today?

- Positive Affirmation for the Day:

- Positive Quote for the Day:

- Write one compliment you can give yourself today.

What are you most proud of today?

What action steps did you take today toward your monthly goal?

Rank My Day:

- How would you rate your day on a scale of 1 to 10, with 10 being the best?

  1 ☐ 2 ☐ 3 ☐ 4 ☐ 5 ☐ 6 ☐ 7 ☐ 8 ☐ 9 ☐ 10 ☐

Because: _____

Tuesday: Daily Check-in

Date: ....

- What are you grateful for today?
  1. ------------------------
  2. ------------------------
  3. ------------------------
  4. ------------------------
  5. ------------------------

- What are five things you love about yourself today?
  1. ------------------------
  2. ------------------------
  3. ------------------------
  4. ------------------------
  5. ------------------------

- How do you plan to support and care for yourself today?
  1. ------------------------
  2. ------------------------
  3. ------------------------
  4. ------------------------
  5. ------------------------

- How do you feel today?

- Positive Affirmation for the Day:

- Today, I am looking forward to:
  1. ....
  2. ....
  3. ....
  4. ....

- Positive Quote for the Day:

- Write one compliment you can give yourself today. ....

What is one thing you want to accomplish today?

What's one new routine you'd like to start doing today?

Rank My Day:

- How would you rate your day on a scale of 1 to 10, with 10 being the best?

  1 ☐ 2 ☐ 3 ☐ 4 ☐ 5 ☐ 6 ☐ 7 ☐ 8 ☐ 9 ☐ 10 ☐

Because: _____

Wednesday: Daily Check-in

Date: ....

- What are you grateful for today?
  1. --------------------------------
  2. --------------------------------
  3. --------------------------------
  4. --------------------------------
  5. --------------------------------

- What are five things you love about yourself today?
  1. --------------------------------
  2. --------------------------------
  3. --------------------------------
  4. --------------------------------
  5. --------------------------------

- How do you plan to support and care for yourself today?
  1. --------------------------------
  2. --------------------------------
  3. --------------------------------
  4. --------------------------------
  5. --------------------------------

- How do you feel today?

- Positive Affirmation for the Day:

- Positive Quote for the Day:

- What are three good things you did for yourself today?
  1. _____
  2. _____
  3. _____

Rank My Day:
- How would you rate your day on a scale of 1 to 10, with 10 being the best?
  1 ☐ 2 ☐ 3 ☐ 4 ☐ 5 ☐ 6 ☐ 7 ☐ 8 ☐ 9 ☐ 10 ☐

Because:_____

Thursday: Daily Check-in

Date: ....

- What are you grateful for today?
  1. _ _ _ _ _ _ _ _ _ _ _ _ _
  2. _ _ _ _ _ _ _ _ _ _ _ _ _
  3. _ _ _ _ _ _ _ _ _ _ _ _ _
  4. _ _ _ _ _ _ _ _ _ _ _ _ _
  5. _ _ _ _ _ _ _ _ _ _ _ _ _

- What are five things you love about yourself today?
  1. _ _ _ _ _ _ _ _ _ _ _ _ _
  2. _ _ _ _ _ _ _ _ _ _ _ _ _
  3. _ _ _ _ _ _ _ _ _ _ _ _ _
  4. _ _ _ _ _ _ _ _ _ _ _ _ _
  5. _ _ _ _ _ _ _ _ _ _ _ _ _

- How do you plan to support and care for yourself today?
  1. _ _ _ _ _ _ _ _ _ _ _ _ _
  2. _ _ _ _ _ _ _ _ _ _ _ _ _
  3. _ _ _ _ _ _ _ _ _ _ _ _ _
  4. _ _ _ _ _ _ _ _ _ _ _ _ _
  5. _ _ _ _ _ _ _ _ _ _ _ _ _

- How do you feel today?
  ....
  ....
  ....

- Positive Affirmation for the Day:
  ....
  ....
  ....

- Positive Quote for the Day:
  ....
  ....
  ....

- What are three things you have learned recently?
  1. _____
  2. _____
  3. _____

What are you most proud of today? -

Rank My Day:

- How would you rate your day on a scale of 1 to 10, with 10 being the best?

  1 ☐ 2 ☐ 3 ☐ 4 ☐ 5 ☐ 6 ☐ 7 ☐ 8 ☐ 9 ☐ 10 ☐

Because:_____

Friday: Daily Check-in

Date: ....

- What are you grateful for today?
  1. ---------------------
  2. ---------------------
  3. ---------------------
  4. ---------------------
  5. ---------------------

- What are five things you love about yourself today?
  1. ---------------------
  2. ---------------------
  3. ---------------------
  4. ---------------------
  5. ---------------------

- How do you plan to support and care for yourself today?
  1. ---------------------
  2. ---------------------
  3. ---------------------
  4. ---------------------
  5. ---------------------

- How do you feel today?
  ....
  ....
  ....

- Positive Affirmation for the Day:
  ....
  ....
  ....

- Positive Quote for the Day:
  ....
  ....
  ....

Amazing things that happened this week:
1.
2.
3.
4.

What action steps did you take today toward your monthly goal?
1.
2.
3.

Rank My Day:

- How would you rate your day on a scale of 1 to 10, with 10 being the best?

  1 ☐   2 ☐   3 ☐   4 ☐   5 ☐   6 ☐   7 ☐   8 ☐   9 ☐   10 ☐

Because: _____

Saturday: Daily Check-in

Date: ....

- What are you grateful for today?
  1. - - - - - - - - - - - - - - - -
  2. - - - - - - - - - - - - - - - -
  3. - - - - - - - - - - - - - - - -
  4. - - - - - - - - - - - - - - - -
  5. - - - - - - - - - - - - - - - -

- What are five things you love about yourself today?
  1. - - - - - - - - - - - - - - - - - -
  2. - - - - - - - - - - - - - - - - - -
  3. - - - - - - - - - - - - - - - - - -
  4. - - - - - - - - - - - - - - - - - -
  5. - - - - - - - - - - - - - - - - - -

- How do you plan to support and care for yourself today?
  1. - - - - - - - - - - - - - - - - - -
  2. - - - - - - - - - - - - - - - - - -
  3. - - - - - - - - - - - - - - - - - -
  4. - - - - - - - - - - - - - - - - - -
  5. - - - - - - - - - - - - - - - - - -

- How do you feel today?
  ....
  ....
  ....

- Positive Affirmation for the Day:
  ....
  ....
  ....

- Positive Quote for the Day:
  ....
  ....
  ....

What are three kind things you did for yourself today?
1.
2.
3.

Write about one thing that was difficult for you today.
_____
_____
_____
_____
_____

The best part of the day was: _____

Rank My Day:
- How would you rate your day on a scale of 1 to 10, with 10 being the best?
  1 ☐ 2 ☐ 3 ☐ 4 ☐ 5 ☐ 6 ☐ 7 ☐ 8 ☐ 9 ☐ 10 ☐

Because: _____

Sunday: Daily Check-in

Date: ....

- What are you grateful for today?
  1. ....
  2. ....
  3. ....
  4. ....
  5. ....

- What are five things you love about yourself today?
  1. ....
  2. ....
  3. ....
  4. ....
  5. ....

- How do you plan to support and care for yourself today?
  1. ....
  2. ....
  3. ....
  4. ....
  5. ....

- How do you feel today?
  ....
  ....
  ....

- Positive Affirmation for the Day:
  ....
  ....
  ....

- Positive Quote for the Day:
  ....
  ....
  ....

My self-care goals for today are as follows:
1. ....
2. ....
3. ....
4. ....
5. ....

I plan to do the following in order to accomplish my self-care goals today:
1. ....
2. ....
3. ....
4. ....
5. ....

I am looking forward to the following today:
1. ....
2. ....
3. ....
4. ....
5. ....

Rank My Day:

- How would you rate your day on a scale of 1 to 10, with 10 being the best?

  1 ☐ 2 ☐ 3 ☐ 4 ☐ 5 ☐ 6 ☐ 7 ☐ 8 ☐ 9 ☐ 10 ☐

Because: _____

Weekly Wellness & Self-care Log

Mon:	Tue:	Wed:	Thu:
#hours of sleep:	#hours of sleep:	#hours of sleep:	#hours of sleep:
Mood: 😠 ☹️ 😐 🙂 😀	Mood: 😠 ☹️ 😐 🙂 😀	Mood: 😠 ☹️ 😐 🙂 😀	Mood: 😠 ☹️ 😐 🙂 😀
Food: Ⓑ Ⓛ Ⓢ Ⓓ	Food: Ⓑ Ⓛ Ⓢ Ⓓ	Food: Ⓑ Ⓛ Ⓢ Ⓓ	Food: Ⓑ Ⓛ Ⓢ Ⓓ
💧💧💧💧 💧💧💧💧	💧💧💧💧 💧💧💧💧	💧💧💧💧 💧💧💧💧	💧💧💧💧 💧💧💧💧
Self care activity: Workout:	Self care activity: Workout:	Self care activity: Workout:	Self care activity: Workout:

Weekly Wellness & Self-care Log

Fri:	Sat:	Sun:
#hours of sleep:	#hours of sleep:	#hours of sleep:
Mood: ☹ 😕 😐 🙂 😃	Mood: ☹ 😕 😐 🙂 😃	Mood: ☹ 😕 😐 🙂 😃
Food: Ⓑ Ⓛ Ⓢ Ⓓ	Food: Ⓑ Ⓛ Ⓢ Ⓓ	Food: Ⓑ Ⓛ Ⓢ Ⓓ
💧💧💧💧 💧💧💧💧	💧💧💧💧 💧💧💧💧	💧💧💧💧 💧💧💧💧
Self care activity: Workout:	Self care activity: Workout:	Self care activity: Workout:

Weekly Reflection

My Expectations

What exactly do we mean by "expectation"? An expectation is a strong belief that something will occur in the moment or in the future. It is a conviction that someone should or will accomplish something. Meeting your own expectations is as simple as believing in your own ability to exceed them. It is healthy to have high expectations of oneself. The issue is that many of us have expectations that are unrealistic.

It's not surprising that in today's hectic world, we internalize a lot of unrealistic expectations. We have access to visuals of many women who are "doing it all" and appear to be living their best life. As a result, many of us place enormous pressure on ourselves to do or expect more, often without realizing how much we're asking.

- What expectations do you have for yourself at this moment?

- What expectations do you have for yourself in the future?

- Are these expectations realistic?

- Make a list of your expectations in the space provided below. You can begin with "My expectations..." or "I expect myself to..."

_____
_____
_____
_____
_____
_____
_____
_____

Notes/Doodles/Reflection

I am Striving To Reach my full Potential

Monday: Daily Check-in

Date: ....

- What are you grateful for today?
  1. _ _ _ _ _ _ _ _ _ _ _ _ _ _ _ _
  2. _ _ _ _ _ _ _ _ _ _ _ _ _ _ _ _
  3. _ _ _ _ _ _ _ _ _ _ _ _ _ _ _ _
  4. _ _ _ _ _ _ _ _ _ _ _ _ _ _ _ _
  5. _ _ _ _ _ _ _ _ _ _ _ _ _ _ _ _

- What are five things you love about yourself today?
  1. _ _ _ _ _ _ _ _ _ _ _ _ _ _ _ _
  2. _ _ _ _ _ _ _ _ _ _ _ _ _ _ _ _
  3. _ _ _ _ _ _ _ _ _ _ _ _ _ _ _ _
  4. _ _ _ _ _ _ _ _ _ _ _ _ _ _ _ _
  5. _ _ _ _ _ _ _ _ _ _ _ _ _ _ _ _

- How do you plan to support and care for yourself today?
  1. _ _ _ _ _ _ _ _ _ _ _ _ _ _ _ _
  2. _ _ _ _ _ _ _ _ _ _ _ _ _ _ _ _
  3. _ _ _ _ _ _ _ _ _ _ _ _ _ _ _ _
  4. _ _ _ _ _ _ _ _ _ _ _ _ _ _ _ _
  5. _ _ _ _ _ _ _ _ _ _ _ _ _ _ _ _

- How do you feel today?
  ....
  ....
  ....

- Positive Affirmation for the Day:
  ....
  ....
  ....

- Positive Quote for the Day:
  ....
  ....
  ....

- Write one compliment you can give yourself today. ....
  ....
  ....

What are you most proud of today?

What action steps did you take today toward your monthly goal?

Rank My Day:

- How would you rate your day on a scale of 1 to 10, with 10 being the best?

  1 ☐ 2 ☐ 3 ☐ 4 ☐ 5 ☐ 6 ☐ 7 ☐ 8 ☐ 9 ☐ 10 ☐

Because: _____

Tuesday: Daily Check-in

Date: ....

- **What are you grateful for today?**
  1. _____
  2. _____
  3. _____
  4. _____
  5. _____

- **What are five things you love about yourself today?**
  1. _____
  2. _____
  3. _____
  4. _____
  5. _____

- **How do you plan to support and care for yourself today?**
  1. _____
  2. _____
  3. _____
  4. _____
  5. _____

- **How do you feel today?**
  ....
  ....
  ....

- **Positive Affirmation for the Day:**
  ....
  ....
  ....

- **Today, I am looking forward to:**
  1. ....
  ....
  2. ....
  ....
  3. ....
  ....
  4. ....
  ....

- **Positive Quote for the Day:**
  ....
  ....
  ....

- **Write one compliment you can give yourself today.** ....
  ....
  ....

What is one thing you want to accomplish today?

What's one new routine you'd like to start doing today?

Rank My Day:

- How would you rate your day on a scale of 1 to 10, with 10 being the best?

  1 ☐ 2 ☐ 3 ☐ 4 ☐ 5 ☐ 6 ☐ 7 ☐ 8 ☐ 9 ☐ 10 ☐

Because: _____

Wednesday: Daily Check-in

Date: ....

- What are you grateful for today?
  1. ....
  2. ....
  3. ....
  4. ....
  5. ....

- What are five things you love about yourself today?
  1. ....
  2. ....
  3. ....
  4. ....
  5. ....

- How do you plan to support and care for yourself today?
  1. ....
  2. ....
  3. ....
  4. ....
  5. ....

- How do you feel today?
  ....
  ....
  ....

- Positive Affirmation for the Day:
  ....
  ....
  ....

- Positive Quote for the Day:
  ....
  ....
  ....

- What are three good things you did for yourself today?
  1. _____
  2. _____
  3. _____

Rank My Day:

- How would you rate your day on a scale of 1 to 10, with 10 being the best?

  1 ☐ 2 ☐ 3 ☐ 4 ☐ 5 ☐ 6 ☐ 7 ☐ 8 ☐ 9 ☐ 10 ☐

Because: _____

Thursday: Daily Check-in

Date: ....

- What are you grateful for today?
  1. _ _ _ _ _ _ _ _ _ _ _ _ _ _ _
  2. _ _ _ _ _ _ _ _ _ _ _ _ _ _ _
  3. _ _ _ _ _ _ _ _ _ _ _ _ _ _ _
  4. _ _ _ _ _ _ _ _ _ _ _ _ _ _ _
  5. _ _ _ _ _ _ _ _ _ _ _ _ _ _ _

- What are five things you love about yourself today?
  1. _ _ _ _ _ _ _ _ _ _ _ _ _ _ _
  2. _ _ _ _ _ _ _ _ _ _ _ _ _ _ _
  3. _ _ _ _ _ _ _ _ _ _ _ _ _ _ _
  4. _ _ _ _ _ _ _ _ _ _ _ _ _ _ _
  5. _ _ _ _ _ _ _ _ _ _ _ _ _ _ _

- How do you plan to support and care for yourself today?
  1. _ _ _ _ _ _ _ _ _ _ _ _ _ _ _
  2. _ _ _ _ _ _ _ _ _ _ _ _ _ _ _
  3. _ _ _ _ _ _ _ _ _ _ _ _ _ _ _
  4. _ _ _ _ _ _ _ _ _ _ _ _ _ _ _
  5. _ _ _ _ _ _ _ _ _ _ _ _ _ _ _

- How do you feel today?
  ....
  ....
  ....

- Positive Affirmation for the Day:
  ....
  ....
  ....

- Positive Quote for the Day:
  ....
  ....
  ....

- What are three things you have learned recently?
  1. _____
  2. _____
  3. _____

What are you most proud of today? _

Rank My Day:
- How would you rate your day on a scale of 1 to 10, with 10 being the best?
  1 ☐ 2 ☐ 3 ☐ 4 ☐ 5 ☐ 6 ☐ 7 ☐ 8 ☐ 9 ☐ 10 ☐

Because:_____

Friday: Daily Check-in

Date: ....

- What are you grateful for today?
  1. ....
  2. ....
  3. ....
  4. ....
  5. ....

- What are five things you love about yourself today?
  1. ....
  2. ....
  3. ....
  4. ....
  5. ....

- How do you plan to support and care for yourself today?
  1. ....
  2. ....
  3. ....
  4. ....
  5. ....

- How do you feel today?
  ....
  ....
  ....

- Positive Affirmation for the Day:
  ....
  ....
  ....

- Positive Quote for the Day:
  ....
  ....
  ....

Amazing things that happened this week:
1.
2.
3.
4.

What action steps did you take today toward your monthly goal?
1.
2.
3.

Rank My Day:
- How would you rate your day on a scale of 1 to 10, with 10 being the best?
  1 ☐ 2 ☐ 3 ☐ 4 ☐ 5 ☐ 6 ☐ 7 ☐ 8 ☐ 9 ☐ 10 ☐

Because: _____

Saturday: Daily Check-in

Date: ....

- What are you grateful for today?
  1. - - - - - - - - - - - - -
  2. - - - - - - - - - - - - -
  3. - - - - - - - - - - - - -
  4. - - - - - - - - - - - - -
  5. - - - - - - - - - - - - -

- What are five things you love about yourself today?
  1. - - - - - - - - - - - - -
  2. - - - - - - - - - - - - -
  3. - - - - - - - - - - - - -
  4. - - - - - - - - - - - - -
  5. - - - - - - - - - - - - -

- How do you plan to support and care for yourself today?
  1. - - - - - - - - - - - - -
  2. - - - - - - - - - - - - -
  3. - - - - - - - - - - - - -
  4. - - - - - - - - - - - - -
  5. - - - - - - - - - - - - -

- How do you feel today?
  ....
  ....
  ....

- Positive Affirmation for the Day:
  ....
  ....
  ....

- Positive Quote for the Day:
  ....
  ....
  ....

What are three kind things you did for yourself today?
1.
2.
3.

Write about one thing that was difficult for you today.
_____
_____
_____
_____
_____

The best part of the day was: _____

Rank My Day:
- How would you rate your day on a scale of 1 to 10, with 10 being the best?
  1 2 3 4 5 6 7 8 9 10
  ☐ ☐ ☐ ☐ ☐ ☐ ☐ ☐ ☐ ☐

Because: _____

Sunday: Daily Check-in

Date: ....

- What are you grateful for today?
  1. _ _ _ _ _ _ _ _ _ _ _ _
  2. _ _ _ _ _ _ _ _ _ _ _ _
  3. _ _ _ _ _ _ _ _ _ _ _ _
  4. _ _ _ _ _ _ _ _ _ _ _ _
  5. _ _ _ _ _ _ _ _ _ _ _ _

- What are five things you love about yourself today?
  1. _ _ _ _ _ _ _ _ _ _ _ _
  2. _ _ _ _ _ _ _ _ _ _ _ _
  3. _ _ _ _ _ _ _ _ _ _ _ _
  4. _ _ _ _ _ _ _ _ _ _ _ _
  5. _ _ _ _ _ _ _ _ _ _ _ _

- How do you plan to support and care for yourself today?
  1. _ _ _ _ _ _ _ _ _ _ _ _
  2. _ _ _ _ _ _ _ _ _ _ _ _
  3. _ _ _ _ _ _ _ _ _ _ _ _
  4. _ _ _ _ _ _ _ _ _ _ _ _
  5. _ _ _ _ _ _ _ _ _ _ _ _

- How do you feel today?
  ....
  ....
  ....

- Positive Affirmation for the Day:
  ....
  ....
  ....

- Positive Quote for the Day:
  ....
  ....
  ....

My self-care goals for today are as follows:
1. _ _ _ _ _ _ _ _ _ _ _ _
2. _ _ _ _ _ _ _ _ _ _ _ _
3. _ _ _ _ _ _ _ _ _ _ _ _
4. _ _ _ _ _ _ _ _ _ _ _ _
5. _ _ _ _ _ _ _ _ _ _ _ _

I plan to do the following in order to accomplish my self-care goals today:
1. _ _ _ _ _ _ _ _ _ _ _ _
2. _ _ _ _ _ _ _ _ _ _ _ _
3. _ _ _ _ _ _ _ _ _ _ _ _
4. _ _ _ _ _ _ _ _ _ _ _ _
5. _ _ _ _ _ _ _ _ _ _ _ _

I am looking forward to the following today:
1. _ _ _ _ _ _ _ _ _ _ _ _
2. _ _ _ _ _ _ _ _ _ _ _ _
3. _ _ _ _ _ _ _ _ _ _ _ _
4. _ _ _ _ _ _ _ _ _ _ _ _
5. _ _ _ _ _ _ _ _ _ _ _ _

Rank My Day:
- How would you rate your day on a scale of 1 to 10, with 10 being the best?

  1 ☐ 2 ☐ 3 ☐ 4 ☐ 5 ☐ 6 ☐ 7 ☐ 8 ☐ 9 ☐ 10 ☐

Because:_____

Weekly Wellness & Self-care Log

Mon:	Tue:	Wed:	Thu:
#hours of sleep:	#hours of sleep:	#hours of sleep:	#hours of sleep:
Mood: 😠 😟 😐 🙂 😃	Mood: 😠 😟 😐 🙂 😃	Mood: 😠 😟 😐 🙂 😃	Mood: 😠 😟 😐 🙂 😃
Food: Ⓑ Ⓛ Ⓢ Ⓓ	Food: Ⓑ Ⓛ Ⓢ Ⓓ	Food: Ⓑ Ⓛ Ⓢ Ⓓ	Food: Ⓑ Ⓛ Ⓢ Ⓓ
💧💧💧💧 💧💧💧💧	💧💧💧💧 💧💧💧💧	💧💧💧💧 💧💧💧💧	💧💧💧💧 💧💧💧💧
Self care activity: Workout:	Self care activity: Workout:	Self care activity: Workout:	Self care activity: Workout:

Weekly Wellness & Self-care Log

Fri:	Sat:	Sun:
#hours of sleep:	#hours of sleep:	#hours of sleep:
Mood: 😟 😕 😐 🙂 😀	Mood: 😟 😕 😐 🙂 😀	Mood: 😟 😕 😐 🙂 😀
Food: Ⓑ Ⓛ Ⓢ Ⓓ	Food: Ⓑ Ⓛ Ⓢ Ⓓ	Food: Ⓑ Ⓛ Ⓢ Ⓓ
💧💧💧💧 💧💧💧💧	💧💧💧💧 💧💧💧💧	💧💧💧💧 💧💧💧💧
Self care activity: Workout:	Self care activity: Workout:	Self care activity: Workout:

Weekly Reflection

My Self-care

Self-care encompasses anything one does on a regular basis to better one's physical and mental well-being, whether it is a hobby, a ritual, or a routine. When you take care of yourself by doing healthy things; managing your illness; and seeking medical, dental, or mental health care when needed, you are performing self-care. Individuals practice self-care every day by maintaining their nutrition, hygiene, exercise, and sleep, and by making time for themselves. Self-care requires consistent effort.

- How can you make room in your daily schedule to focus on yourself? Will you have to give up anything? What will that be? Do you think it will be worthwhile?

- Describe some of your favorite ways to relax and refuel.

- What would you do if you were permitted to dedicate one day every week to self-care? _____
_____
_____
_____

- What prevents you from devoting one day per week to yourself?
_____
_____
_____
_____

Notes/Doodles/Reflection

Monday: Daily Check-in

Date: ....

- What are you grateful for today?
  1. _ _ _ _ _ _ _ _ _ _ _ _ _ _
  2. _ _ _ _ _ _ _ _ _ _ _ _ _ _
  3. _ _ _ _ _ _ _ _ _ _ _ _ _ _
  4. _ _ _ _ _ _ _ _ _ _ _ _ _ _
  5. _ _ _ _ _ _ _ _ _ _ _ _ _ _

- What are five things you love about yourself today?
  1. _ _ _ _ _ _ _ _ _ _ _ _ _ _
  2. _ _ _ _ _ _ _ _ _ _ _ _ _ _
  3. _ _ _ _ _ _ _ _ _ _ _ _ _ _
  4. _ _ _ _ _ _ _ _ _ _ _ _ _ _
  5. _ _ _ _ _ _ _ _ _ _ _ _ _ _

- How do you plan to support and care for yourself today?
  1. _ _ _ _ _ _ _ _ _ _ _ _ _ _
  2. _ _ _ _ _ _ _ _ _ _ _ _ _ _
  3. _ _ _ _ _ _ _ _ _ _ _ _ _ _
  4. _ _ _ _ _ _ _ _ _ _ _ _ _ _
  5. _ _ _ _ _ _ _ _ _ _ _ _ _ _

- How do you feel today?
  ....
  ....
  ....

- Positive Affirmation for the Day:
  ....
  ....
  ....

- Positive Quote for the Day:
  ....
  ....
  ....

- Write one compliment you can give yourself today. ....
  ....
  ....

What are you most proud of today?

What action steps did you take today toward your monthly goal?

Rank My Day:

- How would you rate your day on a scale of 1 to 10, with 10 being the best?

  1 ☐ 2 ☐ 3 ☐ 4 ☐ 5 ☐ 6 ☐ 7 ☐ 8 ☐ 9 ☐ 10 ☐

Because: _____

Tuesday: Daily Check-in

Date: ....

- What are you grateful for today?
  1. ------------------------
  2. ------------------------
  3. ------------------------
  4. ------------------------
  5. ------------------------

- What are five things you love about yourself today?
  1. ------------------------
  2. ------------------------
  3. ------------------------
  4. ------------------------
  5. ------------------------

- How do you plan to support and care for yourself today?
  1. ------------------------
  2. ------------------------
  3. ------------------------
  4. ------------------------
  5. ------------------------

- How do you feel today?
  ....
  ....
  ....

- Positive Affirmation for the Day:
  ....
  ....
  ....

- Today, I am looking forward to:
  1. ....
  2. ....
  3. ....
  4. ....

- Positive Quote for the Day:
  ....
  ....
  ....

- Write one compliment you can give yourself today. ....
  ....
  ....

What is one thing you want to accomplish today?

What's one new routine you'd like to start doing today?

Rank My Day:

- How would you rate your day on a scale of 1 to 10, with 10 being the best?

  1 ☐ 2 ☐ 3 ☐ 4 ☐ 5 ☐ 6 ☐ 7 ☐ 8 ☐ 9 ☐ 10 ☐

Because:_____

Wednesday: Daily Check-in

Date: ....

- What are you grateful for today?
  1. _____
  2. _____
  3. _____
  4. _____
  5. _____

- What are five things you love about yourself today?
  1. _____
  2. _____
  3. _____
  4. _____
  5. _____

- How do you plan to support and care for yourself today?
  1. _____
  2. _____
  3. _____
  4. _____
  5. _____

- How do you feel today?
  ....
  ....
  ....

- Positive Affirmation for the Day:
  ....
  ....
  ....

- Positive Quote for the Day:
  ....
  ....
  ....

- What are three good things you did for yourself today?
  1. _____
  2. _____
  3. _____

Rank My Day:

- How would you rate your day on a scale of 1 to 10, with 10 being the best?

  1 ☐ 2 ☐ 3 ☐ 4 ☐ 5 ☐ 6 ☐ 7 ☐ 8 ☐ 9 ☐ 10 ☐

Because: _____

Thursday: Daily Check-in

Date: ....

- What are you grateful for today?
  1. _____
  2. _____
  3. _____
  4. _____
  5. _____

- What are five things you love about yourself today?
  1. _____
  2. _____
  3. _____
  4. _____
  5. _____

- How do you plan to support and care for yourself today?
  1. _____
  2. _____
  3. _____
  4. _____
  5. _____

- How do you feel today?
  ....
  ....
  ....

- Positive Affirmation for the Day:
  ....
  ....
  ....

- Positive Quote for the Day:
  ....
  ....
  ....

- What are three things you have learned recently?
  1. _____
  2. _____
  3. _____

What are you most proud of today? _____
_____

Rank My Day:

- How would you rate your day on a scale of 1 to 10, with 10 being the best?

  1 ☐ 2 ☐ 3 ☐ 4 ☐ 5 ☐ 6 ☐ 7 ☐ 8 ☐ 9 ☐ 10 ☐

Because: _____

Friday: Daily Check-in

Date: ....

- What are you grateful for today?
  1. - - - - - - - - - - - - - - - - - -
  2. - - - - - - - - - - - - - - - - - -
  3. - - - - - - - - - - - - - - - - - -
  4. - - - - - - - - - - - - - - - - - -
  5. - - - - - - - - - - - - - - - - - -

- What are five things you love about yourself today?
  1. - - - - - - - - - - - - - - - - - -
  2. - - - - - - - - - - - - - - - - - -
  3. - - - - - - - - - - - - - - - - - -
  4. - - - - - - - - - - - - - - - - - -
  5. - - - - - - - - - - - - - - - - - -

- How do you plan to support and care for yourself today?
  1. - - - - - - - - - - - - - - - - - -
  2. - - - - - - - - - - - - - - - - - -
  3. - - - - - - - - - - - - - - - - - -
  4. - - - - - - - - - - - - - - - - - -
  5. - - - - - - - - - - - - - - - - - -

- How do you feel today?
  ....
  ....
  ....

- Positive Affirmation for the Day:
  ....
  ....
  ....

- Positive Quote for the Day:
  ....
  ....
  ....

Amazing things that happened this week:
1.
2.
3.
4.

What action steps did you take today toward your monthly goal?
1.
2.
3.

Rank My Day:
- How would you rate your day on a scale of 1 to 10, with 10 being the best?

  1 ☐ 2 ☐ 3 ☐ 4 ☐ 5 ☐ 6 ☐ 7 ☐ 8 ☐ 9 ☐ 10 ☐

Because: _____

Saturday: Daily Check-in

Date: ....

- What are you grateful for today?
  1. _ _ _ _ _ _ _ _ _ _ _ _ _ _ _
  2. _ _ _ _ _ _ _ _ _ _ _ _ _ _ _
  3. _ _ _ _ _ _ _ _ _ _ _ _ _ _ _
  4. _ _ _ _ _ _ _ _ _ _ _ _ _ _ _
  5. _ _ _ _ _ _ _ _ _ _ _ _ _ _ _

- What are five things you love about yourself today?
  1. _ _ _ _ _ _ _ _ _ _ _ _ _ _ _
  2. _ _ _ _ _ _ _ _ _ _ _ _ _ _ _
  3. _ _ _ _ _ _ _ _ _ _ _ _ _ _ _
  4. _ _ _ _ _ _ _ _ _ _ _ _ _ _ _
  5. _ _ _ _ _ _ _ _ _ _ _ _ _ _ _

- How do you plan to support and care for yourself today?
  1. _ _ _ _ _ _ _ _ _ _ _ _ _ _ _
  2. _ _ _ _ _ _ _ _ _ _ _ _ _ _ _
  3. _ _ _ _ _ _ _ _ _ _ _ _ _ _ _
  4. _ _ _ _ _ _ _ _ _ _ _ _ _ _ _
  5. _ _ _ _ _ _ _ _ _ _ _ _ _ _ _

- How do you feel today?

- Positive Affirmation for the Day:

- Positive Quote for the Day:

What are three kind things you did for yourself today?
1.
2.
3.

Write about one thing that was difficult for you today.

The best part of the day was: _____

Rank My Day:

- How would you rate your day on a scale of 1 to 10, with 10 being the best?

  1 ☐ 2 ☐ 3 ☐ 4 ☐ 5 ☐ 6 ☐ 7 ☐ 8 ☐ 9 ☐ 10 ☐

Because: _____

Sunday: Daily Check-in

Date: ....

- What are you grateful for today?
  1. ----------------
  2. ----------------
  3. ----------------
  4. ----------------
  5. ----------------

- What are five things you love about yourself today?
  1. ----------------
  2. ----------------
  3. ----------------
  4. ----------------
  5. ----------------

- How do you plan to support and care for yourself today?
  1. ----------------
  2. ----------------
  3. ----------------
  4. ----------------
  5. ----------------

- How do you feel today?
  ....
  ....
  ....

- Positive Affirmation for the Day:
  ....
  ....
  ....

- Positive Quote for the Day:
  ....
  ....
  ....

My self-care goals for today are as follows:
1. ----------------
2. ----------------
3. ----------------
4. ----------------
5. ----------------

I plan to do the following in order to accomplish my self-care goals today:
1. ----------------
2. ----------------
3. ----------------
4. ----------------
5. ----------------

I am looking forward to the following today:
1. ----------------
2. ----------------
3. ----------------
4. ----------------
5. ----------------

Rank My Day:

- How would you rate your day on a scale of 1 to 10, with 10 being the best?

  1 ☐ 2 ☐ 3 ☐ 4 ☐ 5 ☐ 6 ☐ 7 ☐ 8 ☐ 9 ☐ 10 ☐

Because:_____

Weekly Wellness & Self-care Log

Mon:	Tue:	Wed:	Thu:
#hours of sleep:	#hours of sleep:	#hours of sleep:	#hours of sleep:
Mood: 😠 😟 😐 🙂 😃	Mood: 😠 😟 😐 🙂 😃	Mood: 😠 😟 😐 🙂 😃	Mood: 😠 😟 😐 🙂 😃
Food: (B) (L) (S) (D)	Food: (B) (L) (S) (D)	Food: (B) (L) (S) (D)	Food: (B) (L) (S) (D)
💧💧💧💧 💧💧💧💧	💧💧💧💧 💧💧💧💧	💧💧💧💧 💧💧💧💧	💧💧💧💧 💧💧💧💧
Self care activity: Workout:	Self care activity: Workout:	Self care activity: Workout:	Self care activity: Workout:

Weekly Wellness & Self-care Log

Fri:	Sat:	Sun:
#hours of sleep:	#hours of sleep:	#hours of sleep:
Mood: 😟 😕 😐 🙂 😃	Mood: 😟 😕 😐 🙂 😃	Mood: 😟 😕 😐 🙂 😃
Food: (B) (L) (S) (D)	Food: (B) (L) (S) (D)	Food: (B) (L) (S) (D)
💧💧💧💧 💧💧💧💧	💧💧💧💧 💧💧💧💧	💧💧💧💧 💧💧💧💧
Self care activity: Workout:	Self care activity: Workout:	Self care activity: Workout:

Weekly Reflection

My Insecurities

We all have fears and insecurities; however, if you identify and work through them, they don't have to destroy your relationships. Insecurity is a feeling of inadequacy, or not being good enough, and uncertainty. It produces anxiety about your goals, relationships, and ability to handle certain situations. Everybody deals with insecurity from time to time. It can appear in all areas of life and come from a variety of causes.

- Describe a time when you faced adversity and emerged stronger.

- Put together a collection of inspirational quotes from books, magazines, websites, etc. What values do these quotes represent?

Notes/Doodles/Reflection

Notes/Doodles/Reflection

I am letting go of all *My Fears* and *Insecurities*

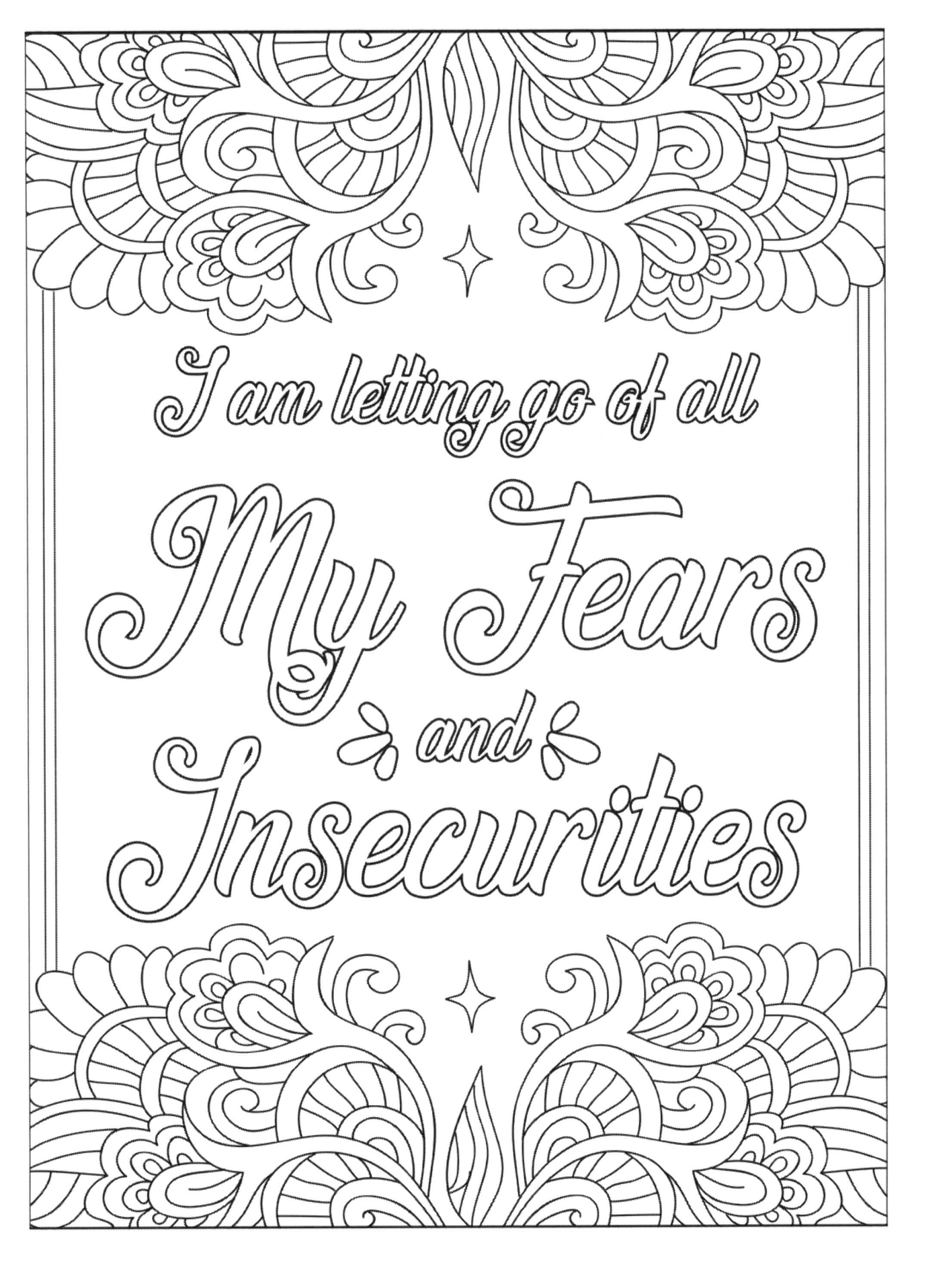

Monday: Daily Check-in

Date: ....

- What are you grateful for today?
  1. _ _ _ _ _ _ _ _ _ _ _ _ _ _ _
  2. _ _ _ _ _ _ _ _ _ _ _ _ _ _ _
  3. _ _ _ _ _ _ _ _ _ _ _ _ _ _ _
  4. _ _ _ _ _ _ _ _ _ _ _ _ _ _ _
  5. _ _ _ _ _ _ _ _ _ _ _ _ _ _ _

- What are five things you love about yourself today?
  1. _ _ _ _ _ _ _ _ _ _ _ _ _ _ _
  2. _ _ _ _ _ _ _ _ _ _ _ _ _ _ _
  3. _ _ _ _ _ _ _ _ _ _ _ _ _ _ _
  4. _ _ _ _ _ _ _ _ _ _ _ _ _ _ _
  5. _ _ _ _ _ _ _ _ _ _ _ _ _ _ _

- How do you plan to support and care for yourself today?
  1. _ _ _ _ _ _ _ _ _ _ _ _ _ _ _
  2. _ _ _ _ _ _ _ _ _ _ _ _ _ _ _
  3. _ _ _ _ _ _ _ _ _ _ _ _ _ _ _
  4. _ _ _ _ _ _ _ _ _ _ _ _ _ _ _
  5. _ _ _ _ _ _ _ _ _ _ _ _ _ _ _

- How do you feel today?
  ....
  ....
  ....

- Positive Affirmation for the Day:
  ....
  ....
  ....

- Positive Quote for the Day:
  ....
  ....
  ....

- Write one compliment you can give yourself today. ....
  ....
  ....

What are you most proud of today?

What action steps did you take today toward your monthly goal?

Rank My Day:
- How would you rate your day on a scale of 1 to 10, with 10 being the best?
  1 ☐ 2 ☐ 3 ☐ 4 ☐ 5 ☐ 6 ☐ 7 ☐ 8 ☐ 9 ☐ 10 ☐

Because: _____

Tuesday: Daily Check-in

Date: ....

- What are you grateful for today?
  1. ------------------------
  2. ------------------------
  3. ------------------------
  4. ------------------------
  5. ------------------------

- What are five things you love about yourself today?
  1. ------------------------
  2. ------------------------
  3. ------------------------
  4. ------------------------
  5. ------------------------

- How do you plan to support and care for yourself today?
  1. ------------------------
  2. ------------------------
  3. ------------------------
  4. ------------------------
  5. ------------------------

- How do you feel today?
  ....
  ....
  ....

- Positive Affirmation for the Day:
  ....
  ....
  ....

- Today, I am looking forward to:
  1. ....
  ....
  2. ....
  ....
  3. ....
  ....
  4. ....
  ....

- Positive Quote for the Day:
  ....
  ....
  ....

- Write one compliment you can give yourself today. ....
  ....
  ....

What is one thing you want to accomplish today?

What's one new routine you'd like to start doing today?

Rank My Day:
- How would you rate your day on a scale of 1 to 10, with 10 being the best?

  1 ☐ 2 ☐ 3 ☐ 4 ☐ 5 ☐ 6 ☐ 7 ☐ 8 ☐ 9 ☐ 10 ☐

Because: _____

Wednesday: Daily Check-in

Date: ....

- What are you grateful for today?
  1. _____
  2. _____
  3. _____
  4. _____
  5. _____

- What are five things you love about yourself today?
  1. _____
  2. _____
  3. _____
  4. _____
  5. _____

- How do you plan to support and care for yourself today?
  1. _____
  2. _____
  3. _____
  4. _____
  5. _____

- How do you feel today?
  _____
  _____
  _____

- Positive Affirmation for the Day:
  _____
  _____
  _____

- Positive Quote for the Day:
  _____
  _____
  _____

- What are three good things you did for yourself today?
  1. _____
  2. _____
  3. _____

Rank My Day:

- How would you rate your day on a scale of 1 to 10, with 10 being the best?

  1 ☐ 2 ☐ 3 ☐ 4 ☐ 5 ☐ 6 ☐ 7 ☐ 8 ☐ 9 ☐ 10 ☐

Because: _____

Thursday: Daily Check-in

Date: ....

- What are you grateful for today?
  1. _ _ _ _ _ _ _ _ _ _ _ _ _ _ _
  2. _ _ _ _ _ _ _ _ _ _ _ _ _ _ _
  3. _ _ _ _ _ _ _ _ _ _ _ _ _ _ _
  4. _ _ _ _ _ _ _ _ _ _ _ _ _ _ _
  5. _ _ _ _ _ _ _ _ _ _ _ _ _ _ _

- What are five things you love about yourself today?
  1. _ _ _ _ _ _ _ _ _ _ _ _ _ _ _
  2. _ _ _ _ _ _ _ _ _ _ _ _ _ _ _
  3. _ _ _ _ _ _ _ _ _ _ _ _ _ _ _
  4. _ _ _ _ _ _ _ _ _ _ _ _ _ _ _
  5. _ _ _ _ _ _ _ _ _ _ _ _ _ _ _

- How do you plan to support and care for yourself today?
  1. _ _ _ _ _ _ _ _ _ _ _ _ _ _ _
  2. _ _ _ _ _ _ _ _ _ _ _ _ _ _ _
  3. _ _ _ _ _ _ _ _ _ _ _ _ _ _ _
  4. _ _ _ _ _ _ _ _ _ _ _ _ _ _ _
  5. _ _ _ _ _ _ _ _ _ _ _ _ _ _ _

- How do you feel today?

- Positive Affirmation for the Day:

- Positive Quote for the Day:

- What are three things you have learned recently?
  1. _____
  2. _____
  3. _____

What are you most proud of today? _

Rank My Day:

- How would you rate your day on a scale of 1 to 10, with 10 being the best?

  1 ☐ 2 ☐ 3 ☐ 4 ☐ 5 ☐ 6 ☐ 7 ☐ 8 ☐ 9 ☐ 10 ☐

Because:_____

Friday: Daily Check-in

Date: ....

- What are you grateful for today?
  1. - - - - - - - - - - - - - - - -
  2. - - - - - - - - - - - - - - - -
  3. - - - - - - - - - - - - - - - -
  4. - - - - - - - - - - - - - - - -
  5. - - - - - - - - - - - - - - - -

- What are five things you love about yourself today?
  1. - - - - - - - - - - - - - - - -
  2. - - - - - - - - - - - - - - - -
  3. - - - - - - - - - - - - - - - -
  4. - - - - - - - - - - - - - - - -
  5. - - - - - - - - - - - - - - - -

- How do you plan to support and care for yourself today?
  1. - - - - - - - - - - - - - - - -
  2. - - - - - - - - - - - - - - - -
  3. - - - - - - - - - - - - - - - -
  4. - - - - - - - - - - - - - - - -
  5. - - - - - - - - - - - - - - - -

- How do you feel today?

- Positive Affirmation for the Day:

- Positive Quote for the Day:

Amazing things that happened this week:
1.
2.
3.
4.

What action steps did you take today toward your monthly goal?
1.
2.
3.

Rank My Day:
- How would you rate your day on a scale of 1 to 10, with 10 being the best?
  1 ☐ 2 ☐ 3 ☐ 4 ☐ 5 ☐ 6 ☐ 7 ☐ 8 ☐ 9 ☐ 10 ☐

Because:_____

Saturday: Daily Check-in

Date: ....

- What are you grateful for today?
  1. - - - - - - - - - - - -
  2. - - - - - - - - - - - -
  3. - - - - - - - - - - - -
  4. - - - - - - - - - - - -
  5. - - - - - - - - - - - -

- What are five things you love about yourself today?
  1. - - - - - - - - - - - - - - -
  2. - - - - - - - - - - - - - - -
  3. - - - - - - - - - - - - - - -
  4. - - - - - - - - - - - - - - -
  5. - - - - - - - - - - - - - - -

- How do you plan to support and care for yourself today?
  1. - - - - - - - - - - - - - - -
  2. - - - - - - - - - - - - - - -
  3. - - - - - - - - - - - - - - -
  4. - - - - - - - - - - - - - - -
  5. - - - - - - - - - - - - - - -

- How do you feel today?
  ....
  ....
  ....

- Positive Affirmation for the Day:
  ....
  ....
  ....

- Positive Quote for the Day:
  ....
  ....
  ....

What are three kind things you did for yourself today?

1.

2.

3.

Write about one thing that was difficult for you today.
_____
_____
_____
_____
_____

The best part of the day was: _____

Rank My Day:

- How would you rate your day on a scale of 1 to 10, with 10 being the best?

  1 ☐ 2 ☐ 3 ☐ 4 ☐ 5 ☐ 6 ☐ 7 ☐ 8 ☐ 9 ☐ 10 ☐

Because: _____

Sunday: Daily Check-in

Date: ....

- What are you grateful for today?
  1. ----------------------
  2. ----------------------
  3. ----------------------
  4. ----------------------
  5. ----------------------

- What are five things you love about yourself today?
  1. ----------------------
  2. ----------------------
  3. ----------------------
  4. ----------------------
  5. ----------------------

- How do you plan to support and care for yourself today?
  1. ----------------------
  2. ----------------------
  3. ----------------------
  4. ----------------------
  5. ----------------------

- How do you feel today?
  ....
  ....
  ....

- Positive Affirmation for the Day:
  ....
  ....
  ....

- Positive Quote for the Day:
  ....
  ....
  ....

My self-care goals for today are as follows:
1. ----------------------
2. ----------------------
3. ----------------------
4. ----------------------
5. ----------------------

I plan to do the following in order to accomplish my self-care goals today:
1. ----------------------
2. ----------------------
3. ----------------------
4. ----------------------
5. ----------------------

I am looking forward to the following today:
1. ----------------------
2. ----------------------
3. ----------------------
4. ----------------------
5. ----------------------

Rank My Day:
- How would you rate your day on a scale of 1 to 10, with 10 being the best?

  1 ☐ 2 ☐ 3 ☐ 4 ☐ 5 ☐ 6 ☐ 7 ☐ 8 ☐ 9 ☐ 10 ☐

Because:_____

Monthly Goals and Reflection

Month of: .... **My Focus:** ....

My long-term goal is as follows:

Short-term Goal:

Steps to Take:
1. ....
2. ....
3. ....

What are some of the potential stumbling blocks to reaching your goal this month?
1. ....
2. ....

What resources and assistance do you require to achieve your goal?
1. ....
2. ....
3. ....

How determined are you to achieve this goal on a scale of 1 to 10, with 10 being the most determined?

1 ☐ 2 ☐ 3 ☐ 4 ☐ 5 ☐ 6 ☐ 7 ☐ 8 ☐ 9 ☐ 10 ☐

What will happen if you don't achieve this goal?
....
....

- **This month, I'd like to try:**
1. ....
2. ....
3. ....

I want to do three things for myself this month.
1. ....
2. ....
3. ....

- **Last month, I felt:**
....
....
....

My monthly recap is:

My most important takeaway from last month is:

Undated Monthly Calendar

MONTH OF: _____

Monday	Tuesday	Wednesday	Thursday

Friday	Saturday	Sunday	TO DO LIST
			☐ ....
			☐ ....
			☐ ....
			☐ ....
			☐ ....
			☐ ....
			☐ ....
			☐ ....
			☐ ....
			☐ ....
			☐ ....
			☐ ....
			☐ ....
			☐ ....
			☐ ....
			☐ ....
			☐ ....
			☐ ....
			☐ ....
			☐ ....
			☐ ....
			☐ ....
			☐ ....
			☐ ....
			☐ ....
			☐ ....

Weekly Wellness & Self-care Log

	Mon:	Tue:	Wed:	Thu:
	#hours of sleep:	#hours of sleep:	#hours of sleep:	#hours of sleep:
	Mood: ☹ ☹ 😐 🙂 😃	Mood: ☹ ☹ 😐 🙂 😃	Mood: ☹ ☹ 😐 🙂 😃	Mood: ☹ ☹ 😐 🙂 😃
	Food: (B) (L) (S) (D)	Food: (B) (L) (S) (D)	Food: (B) (L) (S) (D)	Food: (B) (L) (S) (D)
	💧💧💧💧 💧💧💧💧	💧💧💧💧 💧💧💧💧	💧💧💧💧 💧💧💧💧	💧💧💧💧 💧💧💧💧
	Self care activity: Workout:	Self care activity: Workout:	Self care activity: Workout:	Self care activity: Workout:

Weekly Wellness & Self-care Log

Fri:	Sat:	Sun:

#hours of sleep:	#hours of sleep:	#hours of sleep:

Mood: 😠 😕 😐 🙂 😃	Mood: 😠 😕 😐 🙂 😃	Mood: 😠 😕 😐 🙂 😃

Food:	Food:	Food:
(B) (L) (S) (D)	(B) (L) (S) (D)	(B) (L) (S) (D)

💧💧💧💧 💧💧💧💧	💧💧💧💧 💧💧💧💧	💧💧💧💧 💧💧💧💧

Self care activity:	Self care activity:	Self care activity:
Workout:	Workout:	Workout:

Weekly Reflection

My Self-care

Self-care encompasses anything one does on a regular basis to better one's physical and mental well-being, whether it is a hobby, a ritual, or a routine. When you take care of yourself by doing healthy things; managing your illness; and seeking medical, dental, or mental health care when needed, you are performing self-care. Individuals practice self-care every day by maintaining their nutrition, hygiene, exercise, and sleep, and by making time for themselves. Self-care requires consistent effort.

- How can you make room in your daily schedule to focus on yourself? Will you have to give up anything? What will that be? Do you think it will be worthwhile?

- Describe some of your favorite ways to relax and refuel.

- What would you do if you were permitted to dedicate one day every week to self-care?

- What prevents you from devoting one day per week to yourself?

Notes/Doodles/Reflection

I Take Exceptional Care of Myself

Monday: Daily Check-in

Date: ....

- What are you grateful for today?
  1. _ _ _ _ _ _ _ _ _ _ _ _ _ _
  2. _ _ _ _ _ _ _ _ _ _ _ _ _ _
  3. _ _ _ _ _ _ _ _ _ _ _ _ _ _
  4. _ _ _ _ _ _ _ _ _ _ _ _ _ _
  5. _ _ _ _ _ _ _ _ _ _ _ _ _ _

- What are five things you love about yourself today?
  1. _ _ _ _ _ _ _ _ _ _ _ _ _ _
  2. _ _ _ _ _ _ _ _ _ _ _ _ _ _
  3. _ _ _ _ _ _ _ _ _ _ _ _ _ _
  4. _ _ _ _ _ _ _ _ _ _ _ _ _ _
  5. _ _ _ _ _ _ _ _ _ _ _ _ _ _

- How do you plan to support and care for yourself today?
  1. _ _ _ _ _ _ _ _ _ _ _ _ _ _
  2. _ _ _ _ _ _ _ _ _ _ _ _ _ _
  3. _ _ _ _ _ _ _ _ _ _ _ _ _ _
  4. _ _ _ _ _ _ _ _ _ _ _ _ _ _
  5. _ _ _ _ _ _ _ _ _ _ _ _ _ _

- How do you feel today?
  ....
  ....
  ....

- Positive Affirmation for the Day:
  ....
  ....
  ....

- Positive Quote for the Day:
  ....
  ....
  ....

- Write one compliment you can give yourself today. ....
  ....
  ....

What are you most proud of today?

What action steps did you take today toward your monthly goal?

Rank My Day:

- How would you rate your day on a scale of 1 to 10, with 10 being the best?

  1 ☐ 2 ☐ 3 ☐ 4 ☐ 5 ☐ 6 ☐ 7 ☐ 8 ☐ 9 ☐ 10 ☐

Because:_____

Tuesday: Daily Check-in

Date: ....

- What are you grateful for today?
  1. ------------------------
  2. ------------------------
  3. ------------------------
  4. ------------------------
  5. ------------------------

- What are five things you love about yourself today?
  1. ------------------------
  2. ------------------------
  3. ------------------------
  4. ------------------------
  5. ------------------------

- How do you plan to support and care for yourself today?
  1. ------------------------
  2. ------------------------
  3. ------------------------
  4. ------------------------
  5. ------------------------

- How do you feel today?

- Positive Affirmation for the Day:

- Today, I am looking forward to:
  1. ....
  2. ....
  3. ....
  4. ....

- Positive Quote for the Day:

- Write one compliment you can give yourself today. ....

What is one thing you want to accomplish today?

What's one new routine you'd like to start doing today?

Rank My Day:

- How would you rate your day on a scale of 1 to 10, with 10 being the best?

  1 ☐ 2 ☐ 3 ☐ 4 ☐ 5 ☐ 6 ☐ 7 ☐ 8 ☐ 9 ☐ 10 ☐

Because:_____

Wednesday: Daily Check-in

Date: ....

- What are you grateful for today?
  1. _ _ _ _ _ _ _ _ _ _ _ _ _ _
  2. _ _ _ _ _ _ _ _ _ _ _ _ _ _
  3. _ _ _ _ _ _ _ _ _ _ _ _ _ _
  4. _ _ _ _ _ _ _ _ _ _ _ _ _ _
  5. _ _ _ _ _ _ _ _ _ _ _ _ _ _

- What are five things you love about yourself today?
  1. _ _ _ _ _ _ _ _ _ _ _ _ _ _
  2. _ _ _ _ _ _ _ _ _ _ _ _ _ _
  3. _ _ _ _ _ _ _ _ _ _ _ _ _ _
  4. _ _ _ _ _ _ _ _ _ _ _ _ _ _
  5. _ _ _ _ _ _ _ _ _ _ _ _ _ _

- How do you plan to support and care for yourself today?
  1. _ _ _ _ _ _ _ _ _ _ _ _ _ _
  2. _ _ _ _ _ _ _ _ _ _ _ _ _ _
  3. _ _ _ _ _ _ _ _ _ _ _ _ _ _
  4. _ _ _ _ _ _ _ _ _ _ _ _ _ _
  5. _ _ _ _ _ _ _ _ _ _ _ _ _ _

- How do you feel today?

- Positive Affirmation for the Day:

- Positive Quote for the Day:

- What are three good things you did for yourself today?
  1. _____
  2. _____
  3. _____

Rank My Day:

- How would you rate your day on a scale of 1 to 10, with 10 being the best?

  1 ☐ 2 ☐ 3 ☐ 4 ☐ 5 ☐ 6 ☐ 7 ☐ 8 ☐ 9 ☐ 10 ☐

Because: _____

Thursday: Daily Check-in

Date: ....

- What are you grateful for today?
  1. _____
  2. _____
  3. _____
  4. _____
  5. _____

- What are five things you love about yourself today?
  1. _____
  2. _____
  3. _____
  4. _____
  5. _____

- How do you plan to support and care for yourself today?
  1. _____
  2. _____
  3. _____
  4. _____
  5. _____

- How do you feel today?
  ....
  ....
  ....

- Positive Affirmation for the Day:
  ....
  ....
  ....

- Positive Quote for the Day:
  ....
  ....
  ....

- What are three things you have learned recently?
  1. _____
  2. _____
  3. _____

What are you most proud of today? _____

Rank My Day:
- How would you rate your day on a scale of 1 to 10, with 10 being the best?

  1 ☐ 2 ☐ 3 ☐ 4 ☐ 5 ☐ 6 ☐ 7 ☐ 8 ☐ 9 ☐ 10 ☐

Because:_____

Friday: Daily Check-in

Date: ....

- What are you grateful for today?
  1. ....
  2. ....
  3. ....
  4. ....
  5. ....

- What are five things you love about yourself today?
  1. ....
  2. ....
  3. ....
  4. ....
  5. ....

- How do you plan to support and care for yourself today?
  1. ....
  2. ....
  3. ....
  4. ....
  5. ....

- How do you feel today?

- Positive Affirmation for the Day:

- Positive Quote for the Day:

Amazing things that happened this week:
1.
2.
3.
4.

What action steps did you take today toward your monthly goal?
1.
2.
3.

Rank My Day:

- How would you rate your day on a scale of 1 to 10, with 10 being the best?

  1 ☐ 2 ☐ 3 ☐ 4 ☐ 5 ☐ 6 ☐ 7 ☐ 8 ☐ 9 ☐ 10 ☐

Because: _____

Saturday: Daily Check-in

Date: ....

- What are you grateful for today?
  1. _ _ _ _ _ _ _ _ _ _ _ _ _ _ _
  2. _ _ _ _ _ _ _ _ _ _ _ _ _ _ _
  3. _ _ _ _ _ _ _ _ _ _ _ _ _ _ _
  4. _ _ _ _ _ _ _ _ _ _ _ _ _ _ _
  5. _ _ _ _ _ _ _ _ _ _ _ _ _ _ _

- What are five things you love about yourself today?
  1. _ _ _ _ _ _ _ _ _ _ _ _ _ _ _
  2. _ _ _ _ _ _ _ _ _ _ _ _ _ _ _
  3. _ _ _ _ _ _ _ _ _ _ _ _ _ _ _
  4. _ _ _ _ _ _ _ _ _ _ _ _ _ _ _
  5. _ _ _ _ _ _ _ _ _ _ _ _ _ _ _

- How do you plan to support and care for yourself today?
  1. _ _ _ _ _ _ _ _ _ _ _ _ _ _ _
  2. _ _ _ _ _ _ _ _ _ _ _ _ _ _ _
  3. _ _ _ _ _ _ _ _ _ _ _ _ _ _ _
  4. _ _ _ _ _ _ _ _ _ _ _ _ _ _ _
  5. _ _ _ _ _ _ _ _ _ _ _ _ _ _ _

- How do you feel today?

- Positive Affirmation for the Day:

- Positive Quote for the Day:

What are three kind things you did for yourself today?
1.
2.
3.

Write about one thing that was difficult for you today.

The best part of the day was: _____

Rank My Day:
- How would you rate your day on a scale of 1 to 10, with 10 being the best?

  1 ☐ 2 ☐ 3 ☐ 4 ☐ 5 ☐ 6 ☐ 7 ☐ 8 ☐ 9 ☐ 10 ☐

Because: _____

Sunday: Daily Check-in

Date: ....

- What are you grateful for today?
  1. ---------------------
  2. ---------------------
  3. ---------------------
  4. ---------------------
  5. ---------------------

- What are five things you love about yourself today?
  1. ---------------------
  2. ---------------------
  3. ---------------------
  4. ---------------------
  5. ---------------------

- How do you plan to support and care for yourself today?
  1. ---------------------
  2. ---------------------
  3. ---------------------
  4. ---------------------
  5. ---------------------

- How do you feel today?
  ....
  ....
  ....

- Positive Affirmation for the Day:
  ....
  ....
  ....

- Positive Quote for the Day:
  ....
  ....
  ....

My self-care goals for today are as follows:
1. ---------------------
2. ---------------------
3. ---------------------
4. ---------------------
5. ---------------------

I plan to do the following in order to accomplish my self-care goals today:
1. ---------------------
2. ---------------------
3. ---------------------
4. ---------------------
5. ---------------------

I am looking forward to the following today:
1. ---------------------
2. ---------------------
3. ---------------------
4. ---------------------
5. ---------------------

Rank My Day:
- How would you rate your day on a scale of 1 to 10, with 10 being the best?
  1 ☐ 2 ☐ 3 ☐ 4 ☐ 5 ☐ 6 ☐ 7 ☐ 8 ☐ 9 ☐ 10 ☐

Because: _____

Printed in France by Amazon
Brétigny-sur-Orge, FR